Editor's Note

You Need Never Lose at Bridge, the fourth book in the Menagerie series, was first published in 1984. This edition incorporates some major revisions. Three chapters, which inadvertantly duplicated material contained in *Masters and Monsters,* have been replaced with material from Mollo's original magazine articles.

I would like to thank Squirrel for her encouragement and assistance with these projects.

Phil King

You Need Never Lose at Bridge
at Bridge
Happy Days in the Menagerie

By
Victor Mollo

First published 1984 by Methuen London Ltd
First published by B.T. Batsford 2001

ISBN 0 7134 8613 9

A CIP catalogue record for this book is available from the British Library.

Typeset by KEATS, Harrow on the Hill

Printed by Creative Print & Design, Ebbw Vale, Wales for the publishers,

B.T. Batsford,
9 Blenheim Court,
Brewery Road,
London N7 9NT

A member of the Chrysalis Group plc

Editor: Phil King

Contents

Chapter One
Meet the Cast

The Kibitzers' Coming Out Party was going with a swing. A bevy of juniors, who had been watching the game at lesser clubs, had won their spurs and were to be admitted to the Griffins. To celebrate the occasion Oscar the Owl, our Senior Kibitzer, had invited them to meet the members at what the French call *le cocktail*.

With a plateful of caviar canapés before him, the Hideous Hog was in his element. "You'll find, my friend," he was telling an earnest young Kibitzer-cadet with horn-rimmed spectacles and a bow tie, "that we are all winners here. Not a loser in sight," he added with a chuckle, looking approvingly round the room.

"But surely, sir," ventured Horn-rimmed Spectacles, "the winners must win from someone, so there must be losers, too."

"A superficial view," rejoined the Hog. "You must be thinking of the money, which is purely incidental. If people played to win money the game would have come to an end long ago, for by the nature of things, the losses must greatly exceed the gains, if only to cover the expenses. You see the same thing at duplicate. One pair wins, a few others get places, and the rest are nowhere. Yet they come up for more punishment again and again. Why? Because bridge is the medium in which they express themselves, each one doing his own thing, odd though it be.

"Young people twist and ululate and disfigure themselves with pink dye. Their elders collect stocks and shares and china, or else they lecture others and join societies to inflict compassion on the poor. Those with more sense, be they young or old, boost their egos by playing bridge. Casting inhibitions to the winds, they can be crafty and cunning, scheming, hating, gloating, whining ..."

"To thine own self be true," chimed in Colin the Corgi, the facetious young man from Oxbridge, as he passed them on the way to the lobster salad.

"Certainly," agreed the Hog, "Beethoven was quite right, or was it Chaucer? Take the people we know, starting with Papa. You've met my friend Themistocles Papadopoulos, I believe?" Horn-rimmed Spectacles inclined his head. "What does it matter to him if four of his Catherine wheels are damp squibs so long as the fifth showers sparks, stunning all around with its brilliance? It's the admiration, the applause, not the money or the matchpoints, that make his day."

"But surely, sir, he wants to win money just the same," insisted the Spectacles.

"True," agreed the Hog, "but only because he owes it to himself to underline his superiority. But it's by being superior that he wins, not by raking in the shekels, which mean nothing to him.

"His friend, Karapet, is an even better example. Just as some noble families trace their descent to an historic act of brigandage or some glorious massacre, the Djoulikyans treasure the evil spell cast on their house by the witch of Ararat in the fifteenth century or thereabouts. Everything has gone wrong for them ever since, and so it is that Karapet is inordinately proud of being the unluckiest player of our day. He wallows in misfortune, savouring every minute of the agony – when he lands in the wrong contract, when opponents bring home against him seemingly hopeless slams, when his partner plays out of turn. Forever miserable, he is forever a winner, for no one can rob him of his ill luck."

"What about that portly gentleman with the pale blue eyes and large ginger moustache?" asked Horn-rims. "I've seen him play once or twice. Surely he, too, can't be a winner?"

"Very much so," declared H.H., despatching the last of the caviar canapés. "His favourite pastime is counting. The devout count beads, Walter the Walrus counts points and he's just as pious about it. He's an accountant by profession, you know, but he retired before he started practising and now the only joy he has is making out his tax returns. But however much he draws it out, he can't do it more than once a year. At bridge he can count hand after hand, his own, partner's, opponents'. Action all the way."

Warned by a hissing noise behind him, the Hog deftly intercepted the Secretary Bird before he could reach the tray before him. "Allow me, Professor," he said politely, removing the smoked salmon and handing S.B. the plate with the mustard and cress. "That Secretary Bird," he whispered in a loud aside to the Young Kibitzer. "'Hate thy neighbour' is his motto in life and where could he find so many golden opportunities as at bridge?"

Sleek in his shiny alpaca jacket, his long rubicund nose aglow with champagne, Timothy the Toucan bounced past them in the wake of a tray laden with pintado in aspic and *poulet Jeannette*.

"Doesn't he look like a Toucan?" observed the Hog. "Plays like one, too, of course."

"And yet he wins?" asked Horn-rimmed Spectacles incredulously.

"All the time," H.H. assured him. "The meek and humble have yet to inherit the earth, but T.T. has gone a long way towards it. Oozing from every pore deference for his betters, which means for everyone except the Walrus, he reveres in a highly developed sense of guilt. So he gladly takes the blame for everything in advance, knowing that if he hasn't yet trespassed, he assuredly will do. He wins as he sins, his sensitive conscience recording each time a delicious prickly sensation. And what an honour to be punished for his sins by the holiest in the land!"

The Hog looked round the room, searching for the Rueful Rabbit. "Doesn't seem to be here. Probably he's mistaken the day or the hour or the venue. R.R. doesn't pay much attention to detail, you know, but he is by far our biggest winner. He loves the mechanics of the game, reads all the books, studies all the systems and conventions, tries out every gadget. They confuse him no end, but then so does everything else, so he's no worse off trying to be scientific than if he relied on common sense. And just as Karapet gets a thrill out of his endless misfortunes, so the Rabbit bubbles over with excitement every time his blunders turn somehow into strokes of genius. He keeps his Guardian Angel busy, I can tell you."

"I didn't order coffee to follow ten minutes after my Cointreau." The rasping tones of Molly the Mule could be heard across the room as she admonished an erring waiter. "Kindly bring me another Cointreau *now*, before my coffee gets cold."

"Molly! Our rampant feminist!" There was a note of disdain in the Hog's voice. "Another winner for you. She must always be in the right about everything, but that requires someone to be always in the wrong and where could she find so many wrongdoers, and male ones at that, as at bridge?"

Two ice-buckets away, Charlie the Chimp and Karapet the Armenian were engaged in an exciting dual monologue.

"Did I tell you what happened to me on Thursday?" Karapet was saying. "The diamonds broke 5-1, the clubs were 6-0, the ..."

"Just like that hand I was going to tell you about," quickly countered the Chimp, "the one I had at Brighton, when only a trump lead ..."

"... and he ruffed with a singleton trump ..."

"... we were the only pair in the room ..."

Nervously fingering his bow tie, Horn-rimmed Spectacles addressed the Hog.

"And how about yourself, sir? You are a winner, of course..."

"Yes, I am," admitted H.H. graciously, "but then I enjoy the scoring. I don't need anything else to titivate my ego as most of the others do." Dismissing his own role as of little importance, the Hog reverted to his main theme. "You may find us a little larger than life here, but that's only because life is apt, at times, to be drab and dreary. So we infuse some colour into it. We like to see it sparkle," added the Hog, picking up a glass of Bollinger from a passing waiter. "Drink with me to the winners, sir, to the Griffins who never lose."

Chapter Two
The Rage of the Rabbit

The gentle, docile Rabbit was in a rage.

"Please, please," he had pleaded. "Let me sit North. I know that you don't believe in these things, but I've never yet won a match sitting South. I ..."

"I'm not surprised," rejoined the Hideous Hog, remaining firmly seated in the North position, "but if you will kindly concentrate on your cards, rather than on your seat, you may win this one. Anyway it's too late to change."

All R.R.'s entreaties were in vain.

Aware of his technical limitations, the Rueful Rabbit was accustomed to abuse and accepted philosophically the insults of his betters, so long as they insulted him politely. But to be made to sit South for no reason, just because that insufferable Hog wanted to show contempt for his feelings, to humiliate him in public, that was too much.

The occasion was the annual match between the Griffins and the Unicorns and supporters of both clubs were present in full force.

With tremulous fingers the Rabbit picked up his cards.

Game All. Dealer South.

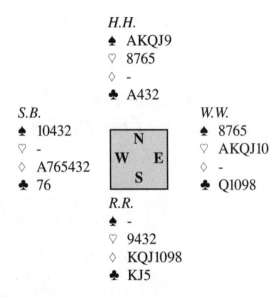

H.H.
♠ AKQJ9
♡ 8765
◇ -
♣ A432

S.B.
♠ 10432
♡ -
◇ A765432
♣ 76

W.W.
♠ 8765
♡ AKQJ10
◇ -
♣ Q1098

R.R.
♠ -
♡ 9432
◇ KQJ1098
♣ KJ5

The Rabbit hadn't psyched more than half a dozen times in his whole life and then only after the third or fourth post-prandial cherry brandy. Never had he psyched vulnerable or first to speak. But this was different for he was determined to teach that Hog a lesson.

With beads of perspiration on his forehead, his left ear twitching nervously, his Adam's apple athrob, the Rabbit tried to look unflustered as in a shaky voice he called, "One spade."

This was the auction which followed.

South	West	North	East
1♠	Pass	3♣	Pass
3◇	Dble	4◇!	Pass
5♣	Pass	6♠	Dble
Pass	Pass	Rdble	Pass
?			

As the bidding proceeded the Rabbit began to fear that he would end up playing the hand in a large number of spades and that though the Hog might be taught a salutary lesson, his own prestige would not be enhanced in the process.

It was too late, however, to draw back. Stoically, he braced himself to pay for his folly, hoping that with any luck he might get out of it for 1100, maybe even 800. The Hog's redouble created an entirely different situation. Disaster was inevitable, but some disasters are greater than others and the Rabbit's one thought was to keep down the cost of this one.

The burning question was: How?

Should he rescue himself by bidding six no-trumps, or maybe seven clubs? Either bid could be misinterpreted and since the Hog was marked with a super-fit in spades for his void, he would revert without doubt to seven spades and, horror of horrors, he might again redouble. That, above all, had to be avoided.

Suddenly the Rabbit had an inspiration. He would escape into seven spades! Destiny had decreed that to be the final contract, but at least this way it wouldn't be redoubled. The tragic message would be unmistakable.

Sighing deeply, with no trace left of his former defiance, the Rueful Rabbit sought refuge in the grand slam.

This time he was doubled on his left by the Emeritus Professor of Bio-Sophistry, known on account of his habits and appearance as the Secretary Bird.

The opening lead was the two of spades.

Muttering dark imprecations, the Hog put down his hand with an angry snarl.

To this day the Rabbit cannot remember in what order he played his cards, but it is on record that after four rounds of trumps he led a club, finessing against the queen. Next he played the king of diamonds then the queen, followed by the knave. For a while S.B. refused to cover, but his ace was trapped and the Rabbit still had an entry with the king of clubs to enjoy the rest of the suit. Five spades, five diamonds and three clubs brought home the grand slam.

The Hog, whose fury had been abating trick by trick, was his old self again as he entered the score.

"Had you been sitting North, R.R., you would have doubtless made an overtrick," he remarked pleasantly.

"Did you have to double six spades and drive them into a grand slam?" hissed the Secretary Bird.

"What possessed you to lead a trump?" spluttered the Walrus indignantly. "A club ..."

"Same thing," broke in the Hog. "Declarer goes up with dummy's ace, draws trumps and taking the club finesse, plays as before. Only by underleading the ace of diamonds can West beat the contract and that's an impossible play. Even I wouldn't find it every time. But cheer up," went on the Hog with a friendly leer at the Kibitzers. "I'm sure your other pair will bid the same way and get the same result."

Vanishing Tricks

In the replay, with Papa the Greek sitting South, and Karapet, the Free Armenian, North, proceedings followed a very different course:

South	West	North	East
Papa	*Toucan*	*Karapet*	*Corgi*
1♦	Pass	1♠	Dble
Pass	Pass!	Pass	

Timothy the Toucan, playing West for the Griffins, was far from certain that he could defeat one spade, but confronted by a complete misfit there was little he could do about it. To leave in the double seemed to be the best of a thoroughly bad bargain.

Colin the Corgi, so named because of his curious shape, began with four top hearts on which the Toucan threw two clubs and two diamonds. Next came a club ruff followed by the return of a low diamond.

Fully expecting the Toucan to have six spades – he was marked with eleven cards in spades and diamonds – Karapet didn't like to ruff. That the Corgi should have no diamonds either came as a distinct shock and a second club ruff completed his discomfiture. One down.

"Their other pair," lamented the Armenian, "will be in five diamonds, unbeatable as the cards lie."

"Curious hand," observed Oscar the Owl, Senior Kibitzer at the Griffins Club. "Played by South with a void in trumps, the grand slam in spades is virtually unbeatable. Played by North one spade is about the limit of the hand, and as we have just seen, even that's no certainty. Maybe," concluded the Owl sagely, "there's something in seats after all."

Chapter Three
The Time Factor

Karapet Djoulikyan was very late. The Free Armenian and Papa the Greek had been drawn against the Hideous Hog and Colin the Corgi in the sixth round of the British Rubber Bridge Championship and the game should have started an hour ago. To avoid having to make conversation with the Hog, Papa sat apart ostentatiously, studying the stop press news in yesterday's evening paper. From time to time, I saw him glance anxiously out of the window. An evil spell had been cast on the House of Djoulikyan in the fourteenth century, or it may have been the fifteenth, and Karapet, who often talked about it, claimed to be the unluckiest of a long line of Jonahs. Papa feared that some expected misfortune had befallen him.

At the other end of the room the Hideous Hog was explaining the facts of life to an eager young man. "You want to raise your standard?" asked H.H. rhetorically. "Then I advise you to improve your cardholding. No, no, don't interrupt me. I know what you are going to say, that the cards you hold depend as much on your partner as on yourself. That is only a half truth. Take my friend Themistocles by the window. He is a great player and when he is dealt an ace he takes a trick with it – well, most of the time, anyway. Now take me. I have only an unsupported king, but I so order things that it takes a trick, just like Papa's ace. So, you see, I have improved my holding from king to ace. Or let us say that Papa picks up five top trumps. Being a fine technician he rarely fails to take five tricks with them. But I can generally extract a sixth, if not a seventh. There may be a squeeze or a pseudo ... "

"Sorry I'm so late," panted Karapet, bursting into the room. "My train travelled in the wrong direction. I booked to Victoria and it went to the coast and I'm not even sure that it started from the right platform. In fact ..."

"What you mean," said the Hog severely, "is that we've been waiting for over an hour because you took the wrong train."

"No, no," corrected C.C., "it was probably the right train. It's just that it was boarded by the wrong passenger."

Both captains, H.H. and Papa, agreed, according to Rule 6, to play for three and a half hours, not to start a new rubber after seven o'clock, but to play to a finish any rubber in progress.

On the first hand Papa made three no-trumps. Then the Hog scored two hearts. This was the third deal.

East/West Game. North/South 60. Dealer West.

```
            ♠ 102
            ♡ 876
            ◊ 1092
            ♣ QJ765

              N
          W       E
              S

            ♠ AKJ9
            ♡ 5432
            ◊ AJ6
            ♣ AK
```

West	North	East	South
Papa	*C.C.*	*Karapet*	*H.H.*
Pass	Pass	1♠	1NT
All Pass			

Papa found the inspired lead of the knave of hearts from the knave-ten doubleton and Karapet took the first four tricks with the AKQ9. The Greek shed two clubs and on the last heart the Hog parted with one of dummy's clubs. The Armenian continued with the ten of clubs.

The Hog had five tricks on top; the ace-kings in the black suits and the ace of diamonds, and he could easily set up a sixth trick in spades. But where could he find the seventh? Before I knew the answer I was called away to make up another table. I learned the sequel later when H.H. was quizzing O.O. in the bar.

"Now then, Oscar, you've lost the first four tricks and you're in with the ace of clubs. You cash the king on which Karapet throws the three of diamonds. Proceed," commanded the Hog.

"Why didn't Colin call two clubs?" asked the Owl to gain time.

"Because," answered the Hog, "we play extended Stayman and Colin didn't want to soar to the three level if he could help it. Besides, he half expected to be doubled in one no-trump. Then he could escape cheaply into two clubs. But that is neither here nor there. You're prevaricating, Oscar. I want to know how you make seven tricks."

"I lead the knave of spades," said the Owl at last. "If it's taken I have an entry ..."

"Of course no one's going to take it," said the Hog firmly. "Dummy's clubs are on view, you know."

"Then, after the knave," pursued O.O., "I cash the ace-king of spades and exit with my fourth spade. If East started with no more than four he will have to lead a diamond presenting me with my seventh trick. How's that?"

"Rotten," replied the Hog. "Why should you assume that a man who bids a spade can't have five of them? And if he has, you're finished before you start. Come to think of it, he *should* have five spades. With a 4-4-4-1 shape he ought to bid one heart, third in hand, rather than one spade on a flimsy suit. No, no, try again, Oscar."

The Owl blinked and hooted softly, but the seventh trick still eluded him. "What did you do?" he asked at last.

"I led the knave of diamonds," replied the Hog. "Just like that." O.O. nodded. "I see," he said. "Karapet is endplayed, for he must either lead a spade away from his queen or a diamond from his second honour. You assume from the bidding, of course, that he started with king-queen of diamonds ..."

The Hog silenced him with an unmistakeable gesture. "He couldn't possibly have the three cards you mention. It would give him a sixteen count and with that much he wouldn't have passed so tamely my one no-trump, not at 60 up, anyway.

"No, I was pretty sure that the diamond honours were split – unless Papa had both. That, perhaps, was too much to expect. But go back to that knave of spades play. You were on the right track and you agreed that it would be allowed to hold, since the ten in dummy was an obvious entry to the clubs.

"The same principle, don't you see, applies to the knave of diamonds. The ten of diamonds is also in dummy and if the king and queen are in different hands, each defender, in turn, expecting me to hold the missing honour, will hold off. And that," added the Hog "is precisely what happened. I made my knave of diamonds and then turned my attention to spades."

The Owl pursed his lips. "I still don't see why my first idea was so bad. I lead the knave of spades, and, if it's not taken, I try your hocus pocus in diamonds."

"Too late," replied H.H. "Once opponents know that you will make three tricks in spades they can't afford to let you get away with the knave of diamonds. That's why you must steal the seventh trick in diamonds before developing the sixth legitimate trick in spades. The order can't be reversed."

"What was the distribution?" asked someone. The Hog filled in the four hands.

C.C.
♠ 102
♡ 876
◇ 1092
♣ QJ765

Papa
♠ 543
♡ J10
◇ K54
♣ 98432

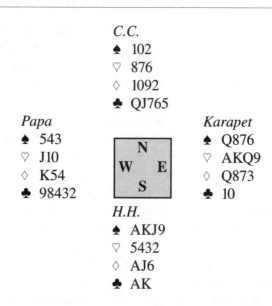

Karapet
♠ Q876
♡ AKQ9
◇ Q873
♣ 10

H.H.
♠ AKJ9
♡ 5432
◇ AJ6
♣ AK

"So," said Oscar, brightening visibly, "Karapet had four spades only, after all, and my way, er, my second way, would have worked?"

"True," agreed the Hog, "but since it would be right for both your opponents to make the wrong play, it would be wrong of you not to allow for the right bid by one of them."

Bold Bidding

I didn't cut out of my table till nearly seven o'clock. By then the match was in the fifth rubber with the Hog and the Corgi leading by 1720. Papa made a game. Then, third in hand, Karapet threw in a balanced seventeen count. It was a good throw-in for only a slam could save the day and after Papa's pass nothing more than a game was in sight. The next hand was passed out, too. Then Papa dealt:

North/South Game. Dealer South.

Karapet
♠ 1098
♡ Q3
◇ AKJ
♣ Q5432

C.C.
♠ 543
♡ J10
◇ 76
♣ AKJ1098

```
     N
  W     E
     S
```

H.H.
♠ 76
♡ 98765
◇ Q1098
♣ 76

Papa
♠ AKQJ2
♡ AK42
◇ 5432
♣ -

South	West	North	East
1♠	2♣	Dble	Pass
2♡	Pass	3NT	Pass
4◇	Pass	4♠	Pass
6♠	7♣	Pass	Pass
7♠	All Pass		

The bidding must be viewed against the background of the overall score. Knowing that Papa and Karapet were hell-bent on a slam, H.H. and C.C. were on the lookout for a desperate gamble. Hence Colin's lead-directing overbid of two clubs.

When the Armenian doubled, the Greek was confronted by a terrible dilemma. Should he leave in the double for a penalty of 300, possibly 500? If so, his side would still need more than the rubber points to win the match. Or should he gamble on finding partner with the right cards for a slam? Of course the odds were against it, but weren't the odds longer still against a better slam hand coming up before the end of the match?

The Greek decided to make a two-way take-out of two clubs doubled into two hearts. If Karapet didn't have the right cards he would stop under game. If his tops were outside the club suit he would march on to a slam. After the Armenian's three no-trumps, which took the auction beyond the point of no return, it only remained for Papa to tidy things up with an inhibitory bid in diamonds. Then he called the predestined slam.

Colin sat back. If Papa made his slam he would score 1630 to win the match by ten points. The cost of seven clubs, allowing for honours, couldn't exceed 1200 and the game would still be very much alive. Colin made the valiant bid of seven clubs and Papa, spurred on by Karapet's forcing pass, took the plunge into seven spades. It was now or never, he felt, and any chance was better than none.

"What's the time?" asked the Greek, as dummy went down.

"Three minutes to seven," replied Karapet, consulting his elegant diamond-studded wristwatch.

Cynics, and there are such even at the Griffins, have ascribed the lowest motives to Papa's innocent question. If the grand slam was on, they hinted, the Greek intended to draw out the play beyond the hour. If the contract was hopeless, he would concede defeat quickly and start the sixth rubber.

The Hideous Hog looked at his watch, screwed his eyes and snarled, but said nothing.

Colin the Corgi opened the king of clubs and Papa counted his tricks. He could see five trumps, three hearts and two diamonds, three if the finesse came off. Should the suit break 3-3 as well, he would have twelve tricks and a heart ruff in dummy would suffice to bring home the grand slam.

Papa shook his head and spoke to himself sternly in Greek. He was probably saying: "It's too much to hope for." Then, smiling, still in Greek, he tried a different approach. Ruffing the king of clubs high, he crossed to dummy with a trump and ruffed another club. Twice more he went over to the table with the ace and king of diamonds and each time he ruffed a club. Seven tricks were in the bag – one trump, four club ruffs in the closed hand and the two top

diamonds. Now he led a heart to the queen and drew trumps from
dummy, discarding two diamonds. This was the four-card end-
position:

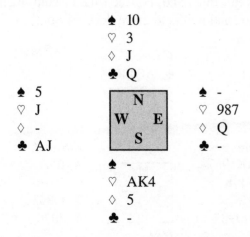

Dummy's last trump squeezed the Hog in the red suits. Had Colin
started with four hearts he too would have been squeezed – in
hearts and clubs.

The Hog Rides Again
Papa beamed. Even Karapet looked less lugubrious than usual.

"Thank you for a very pleasant game," said the Greek. "I make
the difference 790 and," he added, holding Karapet's hand to look
at his wristwatch, "the time is exactly four minutes past seven."

"I think not," said the Hog sharply. "I make it precisely eleven
minutes *to* seven." Oscar the Owl, who was the umpire, agreed. So
did the BBC time signal. So did TIM. Papa asked for TIM twice in
case he had been given the wrong number the first time.

"Sometime," said the Greek, glaring at his partner, "you should
get yourself a decent watch, preferably one with a time-keeping
mechanism."

Karapet sighed. "Everything's against me," he murmured, "it's
the curse. Perhaps that's what happened to that train. It must have
started at the wrong time. Who'd be a Djoulikyan!"

In the sixth rubber Papa and Karapet forged steadily ahead. Both sides made game, but twice H.H. and C.C. sacrificed and before long the difference was 1980. The situation was grim for the Hog when he dealt this hand. For the sake of convenience I have switched the cardinal points to make declarer South.

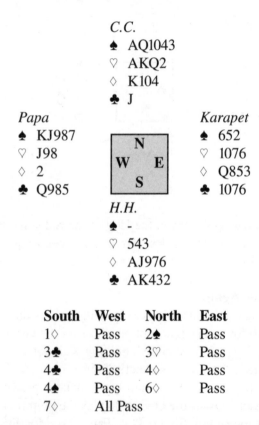

C.C.
♠ AQ1043
♡ AKQ2
◇ K104
♣ J

Papa
♠ KJ987
♡ J98
◇ 2
♣ Q985

Karapet
♠ 652
♡ 1076
◇ Q853
♣ 1076

H.H.
♠ -
♡ 543
◇ AJ976
♣ AK432

South	West	North	East
1◇	Pass	2♠	Pass
3♣	Pass	3♡	Pass
4♣	Pass	4◇	Pass
4♠	Pass	6◇	Pass
7◇	All Pass		

The bidding was simple and straightforward. If Colin could force, the final contract could only be a grand slam, since nothing less would suffice to redress the balance. On the way to seven diamonds the Hog could afford a fancy cue-bid of four spades just to confuse the issue. It meant nothing and he didn't bother to listen to it himself.

To Papa no lead appeared attractive, but a trump seemed the

least injurious and he duly opened his two of diamonds. The Armenian's look of anguish did not escape the Hog, who played the four of diamonds from dummy and covered Karapet's eight with his nine. H.H. laid down the ace and king of clubs and ruffed a club in dummy. A spade ruff in the closed hand was followed by a heart to the ace and a second spade ruff. Crossing to dummy with the king of hearts, the Hog led his ace of spades, throwing a heart from his hand.

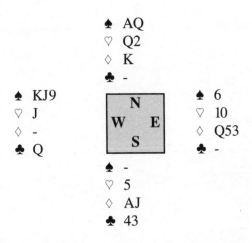

<pre>
              ♠ AQ
              ♡ Q2
              ◇ K
              ♣ -
♠ KJ9   ┌─────────┐   ♠ 6
♡ J   │   N   │   ♡ 10
◇ -   │ W   E │   ◇ Q53
♣ Q   │   S   │   ♣ -
           └─────────┘
              ♠ -
              ♡ 5
              ◇ AJ
              ♣ 43
</pre>

After the ace of spades came the queen of hearts. When Karapet followed, the Hog's features relaxed into a euphoric smirk. He could start counting the chickens for the eggs were hatched. He threw a club and ruffed a spade with the knave of diamonds. The ace and king of trumps scored separately. On each one of the last three tricks – two ruffs, a spade and a heart, in the closed hand and a club ruff with the king of diamonds in dummy – poor Karapet was compelled to underruff.

"Why, oh why did you lead that cursed two of diamonds?" asked the Armenian in martyred tones.

"Top of nothing," suggested the Hog good-humouredly.

"A singleton trump! How could you?" persisted Karapet.

"Not a good lead normally, perhaps," agreed H.H., "but Papa is the man who can afford to do it. Since he never plays true cards on principle, his singletons are dangerously deceptive. I mean, they can't be bare singletons, can they, or they wouldn't be false cards. Ha! Ha! so ..."

"Thank you for a very pleasant match," hastily broke in Colin the Corgi, who was anxious not to miss his train. "Er, what time do you make it, Karapet?"

Chapter Four
Enter Molly the Mule

Though the Griffins is very much a man's club, at the Unicorn, further down Birdcage Walk, where we play duplicate on Thursdays, ladies have always enjoyed full membership rights. Now, in keeping with the times, the rules at the Griffins have been modified to admit members of the stronger sex as guests.

The first to take advantage of this dispensation was Molly the Mule, leading light at the Amazons. The wife of a rich keyhole manufacturer, president of the Free Women's Karate League, Molly is a staunch feminist and a fierce egalitarian, firmly convinced that all men are equally inferior.

Tall, gaunt, with large feet and a long, sharp nose, Molly inspires awe rather than respect. At the bridge table she can hold her own in the most acidulated game – which it usually is when she's around. It wasn't long before she showed her mettle.

An Unusual Trump Squeeze
This was one of the earliest hands in Molly's debut at the Griffins.

Love All. Dealer South.

Karapet
♠ A54
♡ 5432
◇ 52
♣ K1073

S.B.
♠ KQ102
♡ 1087
◇ QJ
♣ Q982

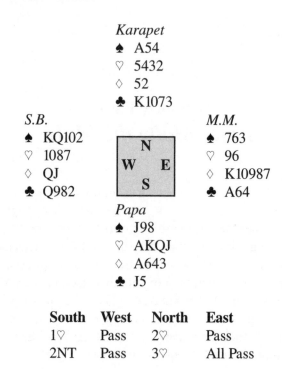

M.M.
♠ 763
♡ 96
◇ K10987
♣ A64

Papa
♠ J98
♡ AKQJ
◇ A643
♣ J5

South	West	North	East
1♡	Pass	2♡	Pass
2NT	Pass	3♡	All Pass

The Emeritus Professor of Bio-Sophistry, commonly known as the Secretary Bird, led the king of spades, which held the trick and, seeing Molly's three of spades, switched to the queen of diamonds, which again was allowed to hold. The knave of diamonds followed, which Molly overtook with the king. Winning, Papa drew trumps and continued with the knave of clubs, covered by the queen, king and ace.

With three tricks aligned neatly in front of her, Molly led the ten of diamonds. The Secretary Bird shed the two of spades and dummy the five of spades, leaving this ending:

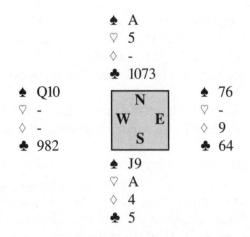

After closely inspecting the trick Molly continued with the nine of diamonds.

As the card touched the table, Papa looked triumphantly at S.B. "Ah, the curse of Scotland, I see. Take your time, Professor. Don't do anything you might regret later."

S.B. hissed in impotent rage. If he parted with a spade, Papa would cash the ace and his knave would be master. If he shed a club, the ten of clubs and a ruff would set up a long club as Papa's ninth trick.

"Why did you squeeze me?" cried the Professor. "All you had to do was to play a spade."

"After you had deliberately thrown the two?" countered Molly. "A come-on card, I suppose!"

"But he had bared the ace, so what could you lose by knocking it out?" persisted S.B.

"I wanted to lock him in dummy," rejoined the Mule. "If I led a club he could have got to hand with a trump to finesse in clubs. I didn't know that you had the eight of clubs, did I?"

"Even if Papa had the eight of clubs," observed H.H., who was kibitzing impartially against both sides, "the finesse would have at best allowed him to exchange one trick for another, a diamond ruff for a club, to say nothing of the clubs being blocked," he added with a chuckle. It was always good tactics in the Hog philosophy to add fuel to a neighbour's fire.

"Extraordinary how men always stick together," said Molly in a loud aside to the empty chair beside her.

"A trump squeeze by East against West. Most unusual," murmured the Owl.

"Surely Themistocles deserves some credit, too, for the, er, sporting way he played the hand," suggested the Hog good-humouredly.

"You, of course, would have made a trick more," sneered the Greek.

"Don't I always?" rejoined the Hog modestly. "You scored eight tricks and graciously accepted the gift of a ninth. I would have made nine all on my own. That's the difference."

A contemptuous gurgle at the back of Papa's throat greeted the remark, but no one asked for an explanation. "Oh, very well," went on the Hog, shrugging his shoulders, "since you can't see it, I'd better dot the i's and cross the t's. Instead of drawing trumps at trick four, after the ace of diamonds, I would lead a club, losing to Molly's ace ..."

"A spade back now is a killer", broke in S.B.

"Molly's return is immaterial," rejoined the Hog. "I come to hand with a trump and lead a diamond ..."

"I can ruff higher than dummy," protested S.B.

"Again immaterial" pursued H.H. "If you ruff, I throw a spade from dummy. One more round of trumps and you have no more, while two remain in dummy to ruff a diamond and a spade. And if you don't ruff the third diamond," went on the Hog, "I ruff, return to hand with another trump and repeat the process. Again, if you ruff, your spade winner disappears. If you don't, you'll get your spade, but no trump trick. Either way, I shall lose no more than four tricks. But, of course, Papa was quite right. With a lady at the table it was more chivalrous ..."

"At the Amazons," broke in Molly, in a rasping voice, "kibitzers are seen and not heard. Next case, please."

Smothering Papa

Molly was well on the way to earning her nickname when, a few days later, this hand came up.

Game All. Dealer North.

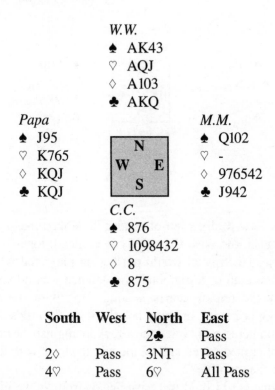

W.W.
♠ AK43
♡ AQJ
◇ A103
♣ AKQ

Papa
♠ J95
♡ K765
◇ KQJ
♣ KQJ

M.M.
♠ Q102
♡ -
◇ 976542
♣ J942

C.C.
♠ 876
♡ 1098432
◇ 8
♣ 875

South	West	North	East
		2♣	Pass
2◇	Pass	3NT	Pass
4♡	Pass	6♡	All Pass

"I have 27½ points and all the controls," announced the Walrus proudly, tabling his hand. "But I left you to bid the grand slam – a couple of kings is all you need."

Papa led the king of diamonds. The Corgi went up with the ace, ruffed a diamond and led a trump, finessing. Dummy's queen held, but Molly the Mule threw a diamond. A knowledgeable kibitzer shook his head. A spade loser being inescapable, prospects were singularly bleak.

The Corgi came back to his hand with another diamond ruff and repeated the trump finesse. Next he cashed the ace-king-queen of clubs, the ace of spades, to which Papa followed with the nine, and continued with the king of spades. This was the position:

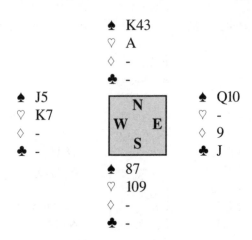

When Papa saw Molly's ten of spades he looked like a man with the death wish, the wish that Molly were dead, for inevitably, on the next trick, the queen would put her on play, and whether she exited with a club or a diamond, the defence was doomed. Colin would play the ten of hearts leaving Papa with the choice of underruffing or having his king beheaded by dummy's ace.

"You smothered me!" cried the Greek in anguish. "Couldn't you jettison that cursed queen and let me win the trick with the knave? Didn't you see my nine?"

"And what card would you have played from knave-nine bare, I should like to know," retorted Molly. "Now had you opened a low spade ..."

"But ... but ..." spluttered Papa.

"One day," persisted Molly, looking at him sternly, "a man will admit that he made a mistake instead of blaming his partner. Obviously that day is a long way off."

"A formidable lady," commented the Corgi when the Mule was out of earshot. "First she squeezes the Secretary Bird, then she smothers Papa. I wonder what she will do next?"

The Mule Meets the Hog
The following day found the Mule and the Walrus opposing the
Hog and the Rabbit.

North/South Game. Dealer West.

R.R.
♠ J2
♡ K2
◊ AKQJ987
♣ J2

M.M.
♠ AQ9
♡ 10543
◊ 106543
♣ Q

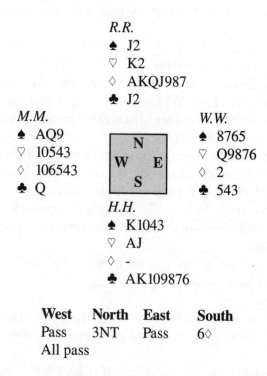

W.W.
♠ 8765
♡ Q9876
◊ 2
♣ 543

H.H.
♠ K1043
♡ AJ
◊ -
♣ AK109876

West	North	East	South
Pass	3NT	Pass	6◊
All pass			

"What do you understand by that bid?" asked Molly when the
Rabbit bid three no-trumps.

"Standard Acol or what's known in the States as the gambling
three no-trumps," replied H.H. "A solid minor and precious little
besides." Whereupon he bid six diamonds.

"And what does that mean?" enquired Molly suspiciously,
turning to the Rabbit.

"Well," replied R.R., conscious that he wasn't good at
explaining things, "it is not in the book, that is, it's in all the books
now, but not when it first started, if you see what I mean."

"I don't," snapped Molly. "What has your partner got?"

The Rabbit thought for a while. "Not diamonds," he said, "no, he has bid my solid suit so as to play the hand which he does so much better than I do. But, of course, in all the books, the new ones, that is, he has tenaces and unguarded kings and queens, so that the lead must run up to him. He must have an excuse, a pretext, if …"

Enough," said Molly firmly, and as behoves a defender with a certain trump trick, she led her ace. Seeing dummy, she continued with the queen of spades. The Hog won with the king and laid down the ace of clubs. When the Mule dropped the queen he switched to the ten of spades, discarding dummy's second club. Crossing with a club ruff, he cashed two top trumps. The 5-1 trump break made him pause for several seconds. Then he led the two of hearts, finessed against the queen, and ruffed another club in dummy. Overtaking the king of hearts with the ace he went on leading clubs. With the queen-knave-nine of diamonds in dummy poised over Molly's ten of diamonds, the story had a happy ending – for the Hog.

"Why didn't you go up with the queen of hearts?" cried Molly. "That would have robbed him of a vital entry and I would have made my ten."

"I don't go in for that fancy stuff," bellowed the Walrus as softly as he knew how. "Your lead gave him the contract, so don't blame me."

"A man will have the last word, if it kills him," was M.M.'s parting shot as she left the table.

"A female chauvinist pig," commented the Corgi.

"Is there such an expression?" asked the Owl doubtfully.

"I don't know," replied the Corgi, "but there is certainly such a person."

Chapter Five
The Walrus Loses on Points

"I had twenty, I tell you," roared Walter, "half the points in the pack! Why, then, should they make thirteen tricks more than me?"

It was not a moment for grammatic niceties. Fate had struck a cruel blow at W.W. and there was both anguish and bewilderment in his voice as he heaved his huge bulk from side to side, like a wounded animal at bay. This was the hand which had seared Walter's soul with shame and his scoresheet with a 2000 penalty:

Game All. Dealer West.

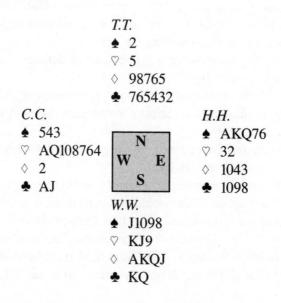

```
                    T.T.
                    ♠ 2
                    ♡ 5
                    ◇ 98765
                    ♣ 765432
    C.C.                              H.H.
    ♠ 543               N            ♠ AKQ76
    ♡ AQ108764      W       E        ♡ 32
    ◇ 2                 S            ◇ 1043
    ♣ AJ                             ♣ 1098
                    W.W.
                    ♠ J1098
                    ♡ KJ9
                    ◇ AKQJ
                    ♣ KQ
```

West	North	East	South
1♡	Pass	1♠	1NT
Dble	All Pass		

Colin the Corgi led the five of spades to the Hog's queen. The heart return, on which Walter played the nine, was won by Colin's ten. A spade put H.H. once more on lead and the two of hearts through Walter's king-knave, allowed the Corgi to run the rest of his seven-card suit. The Walrus had to find four discards. Growing redder and redder in the face he shed three diamonds. Then he came to a full stop and for a moment it looked as if he would refuse to play anything at all.

Finally, after tugging at every card in turn, he let go the ace of diamonds, retaining the knave and ten of spades and the king and queen of clubs as his last four cards. The Hog remained with: ♠ K7 ♢ 10 ♣ 10.

The Corgi's two of diamonds to the Hog's ten, now master, delivered the *coup de grace.*

"Your move, I think," said the Hideous Hog turning to the Walrus with his most engaging leer, "but pray take your time."

Walter the Walrus was helpless. If he threw a club, Colin's ace-knave would win the last two tricks. If he parted with a spade, H.H. would make the seven as well as the king.

"What's the premium for a grand slam in defence?" asked the Hog, chortling gleefully.

"Twenty!" the outraged Walrus kept on repeating. "I had so much to spare that had we not been vulnerable I wouldn't have bid one no trump. I would ..."

"Do you mean," interrupted the Corgi, "that non-vulnerable you would have made fewer tricks?"

His big ginger moustache glowing with anger, the Walrus turned on the Toucan. "How could you even think of leaving me in one no-trump with that shape! You had a six-card suit ..."

"No, no, not a suit, clubs," protested the Toucan "and we are playing Extended Stayman. You might have responded in a major. Then what would I have done? Besides," went on T.T., "if you wanted a minor, why didn't you bid two no-trumps? The, unusual no trump ..."

"Oh! come," jeered the Hog, "you can't complain that it wasn't unusual. Ha! Ha!"

W.W. was deeply hurt. It wasn't only the outsize penalty or the humiliation of failing to take a single trick with so many top cards. It was his faith in the point count which had been brutally affronted. The Walrus believed in points as others believe in goodness, justice or real estate. A pillar of the establishment had toppled. It was as if Imperial Chemicals or General Motors had given him a dud cheque. The Walrus wasn't merely hurt. He was shocked and scandalised.

"Don't fret, Walter," said the Hog mockingly, "you had as many points as we did. The quantity was all right. It was just that the quality wasn't quite up to standard."

A Speculative Double
Two other catastrophes stand out in the series of disasters which stud W.W.'s record over the past few months. The first occurred in a friendly match between the Griffins and the Unicorns. Most of the Griffins belong to both clubs. They play rubber bridge at home, where the stakes are higher, and stroll across to the Unicorn for the occasional duplicate.

Walter the Walrus, captaining the Unicorns, invited Karapet to be his partner. "I am well aware of the evil spell cast long ago on your house," he told him. "Every hand, no doubt, will be bewitched. No card will ever be right. But for once you will know the curse of the Djoulikyans cannot harm you without harming in equal measure your opponents in the other room."

The Hideous Hog, captaining the Griffins, went into battle with the Rueful Rabbit.

"I am giving the law of averages one more chance," announced H.H., "perhaps if I face that Rabbit of my own free will on 32 consecutive boards, I shall not cut him quite so often at rubber bridge."

This was one of the early boards in the match:

Love All. Dealer West.

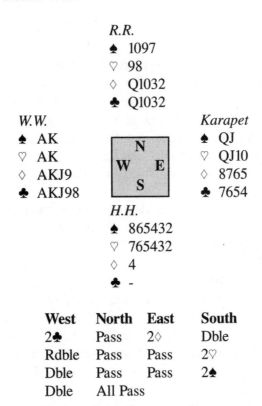

R.R.
♠ 1097
♡ 98
◇ Q1032
♣ Q1032

W.W.
♠ AK
♡ AK
◇ AKJ9
♣ AKJ98

Karapet
♠ QJ
♡ QJ10
◇ 8765
♣ 7654

H.H.
♠ 865432
♡ 765432
◇ 4
♣ -

West	North	East	South
2♣	Pass	2◇	Dble
Rdble	Pass	Pass	2♡
Dble	Pass	Pass	2♠
Dble	All Pass		

The Walrus opened the king of diamonds, then switched to the king of clubs. The Hog ruffed and led a trump. Coming in with the ace, Walter persisted with the ace of clubs, ruffed by the Hog, who led a second trump, crashing the king and queen. The Walrus switched back to diamonds, but after ruffing the ace, H.H. still had a trump left and he couldn't be forced again while he set about the hearts.

Neither could the luckless Walrus avoid making him a present of three discards in the minors – the queen and ten of the suit he now led and the queen in the other, for this was the position when W.W. won his second trick in hearts:

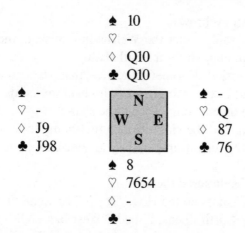

The Walrus would have fared no better had he kept his ace of diamonds and persisted with clubs, setting up the eight. The Hog, it is true, would have had only two discards in dummy for his hearts, but he would have had one trump more to leave this four-card end position:

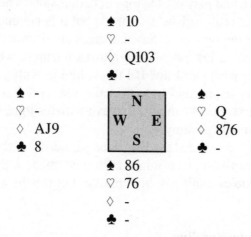

The Hog would have ruffed the eight of clubs in his hand, trumped a heart on the table and still had a trump left to get back and score the thirteenth heart.

"Roughly speaking, 470 to North/South," observed the Hog,

arching an impish eyebrow.

"We had 36," said Walter the Walrus in a hushed, incredulous voice, "more than enough for a small slam."

"I thought," cried Karapet bitterly, "that the curse of the Djoulikyans would extend to anyone who held my cards. Can you doubt that in the other room they bid the slam?"

"Probably," agreed the Hog, "which makes me think that, your luck must be on the turn, Karapet, for your side cannot make game, let alone a slam."

"With 36 ..." spluttered the Walrus.

"Not enough," snapped the Hog. "Try it," he went on. "Against three no-trumps North opens a spade. West has eight tricks, but before he can develop the ninth, the defence get the spades going and that's that."

"They won't play it in no-trumps. Game in either minor must be cold," declared the Walrus defiantly.

The Hideous Hog shook his head. "Even I couldn't make it," he said modestly, casting down his small beady eyes. "I win the spade or heart opening and play off the tops in both majors. Then I throw North in and his return gives me a trick, but it is not enough for I cannot avoid losing two more. Say that clubs are trumps. I play the ace of clubs, then a low one. North returns a trump, which costs him a trick. But what can I do? If I throw him in with a diamond, he plays another trump and lives to make a second diamond. If I draw trumps first, North can afford to exit with his third spade, for no trump remains in dummy.

"For all that," concluded the Hog, looking sternly at the Walrus, "you had a cheap save. You might even have made a part-score. Speculative doubles don't pay in duplicate. Let this be a lesson to you, Walter."

Perfect Misunderstanding

The third catastrophe of the year occurred quite recently at rubber bridge when an American visitor to the Griffins cut the Rabbit against Walter and the Emeritus Professor of Bio-Sophistry, known on account of his appearance as the Secretary Bird.

"What shall we play?" asked the Rabbit.

"At home," replied our overseas visitor, "I play Standard American, but ..."

"No, no," broke in the Rueful Rabbit, "I'll gladly play Standard American. My no-trumps are always 12-14. I play Baron, Swiss, Flint, of course, South African Texas ..."

"I'd much rather play Acol," said the American. "Very much rather."

Each side made game, then this hand came up:

Game All. Dealer South.

```
                    A.V.
                    ♠ 954
                    ♡ A87653
                    ◊ 7
                    ♣ 987
  W.W.                              S.B.
  ♠ AQ1076          ┌───────┐      ♠ J32
  ♡ 9               │   N   │      ♡ 2
  ◊ AQ32            │ W   E │      ◊ 65
  ♣ AQJ             │   S   │      ♣ K1065432
                    └───────┘
                    R.R.
                    ♠ K8
                    ♡ KQJ104
                    ◊ KJ10984
                    ♣ -
```

South	West	North	East
1♡	1♠	4♡	Pass
4NT	Pass	5♣	Pass
7♡	Dble	Pass	Pass
Rdble	All Pass		

The bidding, perhaps, calls for a word of explanation. With three kings and a near-solid trump suit, the Rabbit felt certain that his partner had at least two aces and possibly three. What else could he have for his raise to four hearts? Anyway, it cost nothing to explore, for the bidding could always stop at five hearts, a contract no one could surely break.

The American, for his part, knew enough about Acol to realise that his hand hardly qualified for a raise to four hearts. It was a good, tactical bid over one spade, but playing Acol partner might well expect from him a good deal more. To discourage any further attempt at a slam he decided, therefore, to conceal his ace. Hence the response of five clubs.

The Rabbit was thrilled to the core. He hadn't visualised the possibility of finding partner with all four aces, yet the five clubs response was unmistakeable, for the American could hardly have a hand with no ace at all. In bidding the grand slam the Rabbit felt that he had at least one trick to spare.

The Walrus, who didn't like to be trifled with, doubled in a voice of thunder. The Rabbit redoubled as a matter of courtesy. Not to have done so, he explained afterwards, might have been interpreted by an overseas visitor as lack of confidence and it was far better to risk a few hundred points than to be unmannerly.

The Walrus led his singleton trump and as dummy went down apologies were exchanged briskly across the table.

"My fault, I am not really familiar with Acol," began the American. "No, no, I'm to blame," the Rabbit reassured him. "I, er, misjudged the distribution of the aces."

Thereupon R.R. won the first trick in his hand and promptly led the seven of diamonds from dummy. "Your hand," came like a flash from the Secretary Bird. "A diamond, if you please," he added severely, intercepting a trump before it could hit the green baize.

Shrugging his shoulders, for in reality it didn't matter, the Rabbit led the four of diamonds. The Walrus, after due consideration followed with the two. Having no more trumps, he didn't want the lead for he couldn't tell which ace to play. It was better, therefore, to let the trick run up to partner.

It was a little while before it dawned on the Rabbit that the seven of diamonds had taken the trick.

Before gathering it he waited politely, but no one claimed it. His ears twitching excitedly, he came back to his hand with a trump and led the king of diamonds. There was nothing the Walrus could do to prevent R.R. from setting up three diamond tricks to take care of dummy's three small spades. In fact, he could have tabled his hand after trick two.

"Why did you double?" hissed the Secretary Bird fixing the Walrus with a cold, venomous stare.

"What!" cried the Walrus indignantly. "With three aces you wouldn't double a grand slam?"

"Not if I didn't intend to make at least one of them," retorted S.B.

The American visitor stroked his chin meditatively. "Your Acol is a grand system," he said admiringly. "I know of no other on which we could have reached a grand slam with those cards."

Chapter Six
Unilateral Disarmament

"One day," he told us, "I may be able to eliminate partner altogether. He will just sit there like a zombie, carrying out my orders, without bidding or playing anything on his own initiative. Yes, I have great faith in the future."

"But why shouldn't partner play, too?" protested Oscar the Owl, our Senior Kibitzer. "He pays table money, buys you drinks, surely he has a right ..."

"A right?" broke in H.H. indignantly. "You may as well say that a lunatic has a right to set his house on fire so long as he pays the rates. What if you live in the same house? And how about helpless old ladies crossing roads? Have they, too, the right to get run over or should you take control and guide them through the traffic?

"One has moral obligations in life," went on the Hog warmly, "and though partner may have the right, as you say, to play and bid on his own and to commit suicide, it is your duty to stop him doing it as long as possible, er, till the end of the rubber, anyway."

Two recent hands had given the Hog full scope to discharge his lofty moral obligations. This was one of them:

Love All. Dealer East.

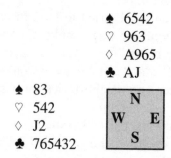

```
                    ♠ 6542
                    ♡ 963
                    ◊ A965
                    ♣ AJ
    ♠ 83          ┌─────────┐
    ♡ 542         │    N    │
    ◊ J2          │  W   E  │
    ♣ 765432      │    S    │
                  └─────────┘
```

South	West	North	East
Papa	*H.H.*	*Karapet*	*W.W.*
			1♡
1♠	Pass	2♠	Pass
3♠	Pass	4♠	Pass
Pass	Dble	All Pass	

"I was West, as you have doubtless guessed," pursued the Hog. "My usual sort of hand. Papa, also as usual, had enough to reach game. A straightforward bidding sequence ..."

"Particularly the double," chipped in Colin the Corgi, the facetious young man from Oxbridge.

The Hog turned on him quickly. "A defender's first duty," he declared, jerking imperiously a fat pink forefinger, "is to do nothing to help declarer. Can you seriously contend that my double would do that? Of course not. And it's safe. After such hesitant bidding no one can redouble and an overtrick is unlikely. Besides, how did I know that the Walrus shouldn't have doubled himself? *Somebody* had to bid his cards."

We went through the play. The Hog opened a heart to W.W.'s king and ace, Papa's cards being the queen and knave. Ruffing a third heart, the Greek proceeded with the king of clubs, a club to dummy's ace and a trump on which Walter played the queen. Papa won the trick with the ace and continued with the knave of spades.

"Well," said the Hog when he had reached this point in the story, "have you beaten the contract?"

O.O. hooted noncommittally. P.P. tried to look inscrutable. "I followed suit conscientiously all the way," said C.C., "but you, no doubt, thought of something better."

"Certainly," declared H.H., "and if it will assist you in any way, I can tell you now that Walter won the third trick for our side with the king of spades."

Oscar the Owl looked sorely puzzled. "Do you mean," he asked, "that with those tram tickets you somehow stopped declarer ..."

"No, no," interrupted the Hog. "I wasn't concerned with declarer. Needless to say, he couldn't make the contract on his own, but I had to stop Walter presenting him with it, which, left to himself, he would have done with alacrity. You see it all, don't you?" asked H.H., fixing the Toucan with a malevolent look.

"Yes, er, yes," replied T.T., bouncing unsteadily.

"Then I'd better explain," went on the Hog. "Papa's hand was an open book. He started with two hearts. We know that for he followed twice. He could hardly have a third club or he would have ruffed it. Spades? With six to the ace-king he would have laid down the ace before touching clubs, so I could tell from his play that he had five trumps, missing two honours – which is why he wanted to lead trumps from dummy."

"Elementary," cooed Colin softly.

"Precisely," agreed H.H., "so elementary, in fact, that even that Walrus was bound to see it. That was the danger. Knowing that declarer had no hearts or clubs left, he would be careful not to present him with a ruff and discard. He would lead a diamond – and present him instead with his unmakable contract. You may as well see the full deal." The Hog filled in the other hands.

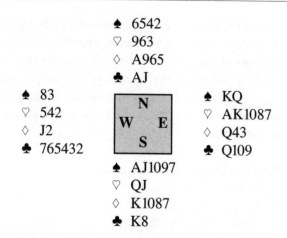

```
                    ♠ 6542
                    ♡ 963
                    ◊ A965
                    ♣ AJ
   ♠ 83          ┌─────────┐      ♠ KQ
   ♡ 542         │    N    │      ♡ AK1087
   ◊ J2          │  W   E  │      ◊ Q43
   ♣ 765432      │    S    │      ♣ Q109
                 └─────────┘
                    ♠ AJ1097
                    ♡ QJ
                    ◊ K1087
                    ♣ K8
```

"I couldn't be sure of the diamond position," continued H.H., "but it was crystal clear that if Papa didn't have the king of diamonds, he would lose the contract anyway and if he had both the king and queen he couldn't fail to make it. So I was concerned only with the actual distribution, as you see it, and my object was to prevent Walter from leading a diamond. Any ideas?"

After a brief pause to make sure that the magnum was empty, H.H. resumed: "Fortunately, that Walrus is eminently bamboozable, for though he knows precious little about bridge, he knows all about points, conventions, peters, echoes and signals of every sort. So all I had to do was to play the eight of spades before the three of spades, proclaiming three trumps and a desire to ruff. Seeing the eight, even Walter could work out that my third trump, the one I didn't have, was the nine. Thereupon he duly led a heart. The ruff and discard were, of course, useless to Papa, who still had to concede a diamond."

"So the helpless old lady was escorted safely across the road," observed Oscar the Owl.

"Chivalrous, as always," remarked the Corgi. H.H. didn't hear him. He was busy scribbling.

The Age of Chivalry

"Here you are," announced the Hog. "You can look at all four hands and play double dummy if you like. And talking of helpless old ladies, you may as well know that my partner was that Rabbit, the luckiest player in the universe. Why, he cuts me three times out of four and when you are at the receiving end, believe me, it feels like four times out of three. He tries to make up for it, mind you, by holding good cards, but then that's the least a poor player can do."

This was the deal:

Love All. North/South 30. Dealer South.

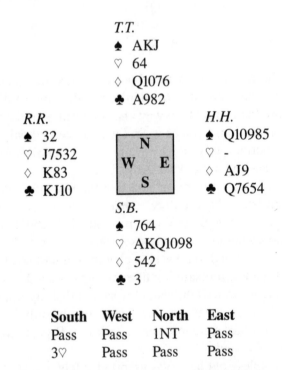

```
                    T.T.
                    ♠ AKJ
                    ♡ 64
                    ◇ Q1076
                    ♣ A982
     R.R.                              H.H.
     ♠ 32             N                ♠ Q10985
     ♡ J7532      W       E            ♡ -
     ◇ K83            S                ◇ AJ9
     ♣ KJ10                            ♣ Q7654
                    S.B.
                    ♠ 764
                    ♡ AKQ1098
                    ◇ 542
                    ♣ 3
```

South	West	North	East
Pass	Pass	1NT	Pass
3♡	Pass	Pass	Pass

"The Rabbit led the three of spades. Sizing up the situation at a glance, the Secretary Bird went up with dummy's ace and confidently led a trump to his queen. When I showed out, he went into a huddle, crossed his long, spindly legs, hissed, murmured darkly about murdering someone in his past incarnation and looked at the ceiling for inspiration.

"Eventually he led a club to the ace, ruffed a club with the eight of hearts in the closed hand and went over to dummy with a spade to the king."

The Hog paused.

"A very good hand," said the Corgi, "and now shall I show you a slam I ..."

Dismissing the offer with a short, contemptuous snarl, H.H. resumed: "Naturally, I could tell every card. Declarer's hearts were so good that he couldn't have another picture or he wouldn't have passed as dealer. He started off jauntily, because he thought he could see nine tricks. Dummy had three, so he was relying on six trump tricks. He ruffed the second club with the eight, presumably his lowest trump, and he won trick two with the queen of hearts, so his trump holding had to be exactly what it was. I could place every pip. You can see, of course, what was going to happen."

As he looked for an un-empty glass, the Hog waited for a helpful question.

"That slam I was going to tell you about, "began the Corgi, "I had the king to ..."

This time the Hideous Hog didn't even trouble to snarl.

"Declarer," he continued hastily, "would ruff another club and exit with his third spade. The Rabbit, who led the three, followed on the second round with the two, so there was no mystery about the suit. But what would R.R. play on the third spade? He would have at this stage five trumps and three diamonds, so he would, of course, throw a diamond and it would be all over. He would be endplayed in trumps. S.B. would have three losing diamonds as before, but the Rabbit with trumps only left, would have to ruff my ace of diamonds and lead a trump into the ace-king-ten."

"Unless you save her quickly from that oncoming bus, the helpless old lady will be run over," warned the Owl.

"Exactly," agreed the Hog. "The Rabbit had to be made to shorten his trumps before it was too late. To be more precise, I had to compel him to ruff that third spade and the only way I could do it was by throwing my queen under the king, so as to promote the knave."

The Hog paused, but seeing C.C. open his mouth, he went on quickly. "Luckily, that Rabbit has learned to observe the fall of the honour cards and he quickly spotted my queen. He concluded, no doubt, that I had a doubleton and that declarer had been dealt sixteen cards. That sort of thing never bothers R.R. So he ruffed the spade and led a low diamond to my knave. I returned the nine of diamonds to his king and was on play at the decisive moment with the ace of diamonds. Having nothing but trumps left, the Rabbit couldn't even revoke and his knave won the setting trick. You see," concluded the Hog, "how carefully I had to play his cards to break the contract."

"You've made out a pretty strong case for unilateral disarmament," observed Oscar the Owl. "Defuse partner, remove his weapons and he will find it that much harder to commit suicide, taking you along with him."

Chapter Seven
Fortune Smiles on the Hog

The Hog was having a good run, or rather, to be more precise, Papa was having a bad one and the Hog was enjoying it. Three hands in less than a week had seen the Greek's discomfiture. The first came up at rubber bridge. Things were going well for H.H. Not once had his partner, the Rueful Rabbit, revoked and only twice had he played out of turn.

With a euphoric grunt H.H. picked up:

♠ A32
♡ -
♢ A54
♣ AKQJ1092

The Rabbit dealt and bid three hearts. Karapet passed and the Hog called three no-trumps. For nearly ten seconds his pink cheeks were creased in a smile. Then, as Papa passed and R.R. called four hearts, the smile quickly vanished, giving way to a scowl. Such bidding simply couldn't exist.

"Four no-trumps," he called angrily.

Insensitive to atmosphere, the Rabbit missed the threatening undertones. All he knew was that his favourite Blackwood had been set in motion and he proudly proclaimed his dearth of aces: "Five clubs."

The Hog was ready for it and he passed with alacrity, consoling himself with the thought of 150 honours.

There was an agonising moment when the Greek doubled. His intention, of course, was to destabilise the Rabbit. Maybe, in a panic, he would try to escape. Papa was willing him to bid. The Hog was willing him to pass. The clash of wills brought beads of perspiration to the Rabbit's forehead. Needless to say, he had no idea of what was going on, but it was clear to him beyond the shadow of a doubt that the Hog was very, very angry. He was frightened of being left in five clubs doubled. He was even more frightened of the Hog. The balance of terror tilted towards passing and in a tremulous voice, with downcast eyes, the Rabbit murmured: "No bid."

This was the deal.

H.H.
♠ A32
♡ -
♢ A54
♣ AKQJ1092

Karapet
♠ KQJ104
♡ K5
♢ Q107
♣ 654

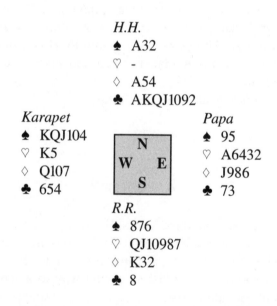

Papa
♠ 95
♡ A6432
♢ J986
♣ 73

R.R.
♠ 876
♡ QJ10987
♢ K32
♣ 8

Karapet opened the king of spades, which the Rabbit ducked in dummy. This took only a few seconds, but it was long enough for H.H. to pour forth a spate of invective.

"Even if you have mixed up your cards as you usually do," he began, "you cannot have a hand to justify such presposterous bidding. It's ..."

"My hand wasn't suitable ..." protested the Rabbit feebly.

"Didn't I hear your opening? Didn't I know what it meant?"

"I ..."

"Get out your abacus. Count your beads and tell me if even you could fail to make three no-trumps."

As he spoke, the Armenian led a second spade. The Rabbit went up with dummy's ace, crossed to his hand with the eight of clubs and continued with the queen of hearts, which Karapet covered with the king of hearts, the Rabbit throwing on it dummy's remaining spade.

Karapet surveyed his options. A spade would be pointless. A diamond could cost a trick. A club seemed to be the answer, for though it would do no good, it could hardly do any harm either. The Rabbit won the trump return with dummy's ace and went into a trance.

Papa fidgeted. Karapet twirled an impatient eyebrow. The Hog snorted contemptuously. What on earth could the Rabbit be thinking about?

Eventually R.R. produced a small heart and quickly followed with the knave of hearts from his hand.

"Did it take you all that time to decide to lead from the wrong hand?" asked the exasperated Hog.

R.R. uttered a group of sounds. The first few could have been: "I trump ..." The rest was totally incoherent. Of course, in the heat of the moment he had forgotten that he was not playing the hand in hearts and he had been trying to draw trumps. It was not his fault. If people started bawling and jeering before the first card is played, what can they expect?

With pursed lips, looking testy, but saying nothing, the Rabbit proceeded to play out dummy's trumps one by one. High cards flashed past him right and left as Karapet signalled and Papa deftly falsecarded. Until the last few cards he was not paying much attention. Then he began to take notice, but it was, of course, too late. This was the position:

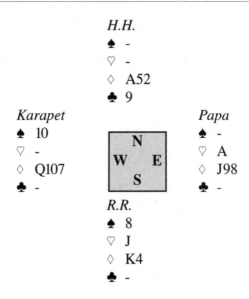

H.H.
♠ -
♡ -
◇ A52
♣ 9

Karapet
♠ 10
♡ -
◇ Q107
♣ -

Papa
♠ -
♡ A
◇ J98
♣ -

R.R.
♠ 8
♡ J
◇ K4
♣ -

As he led dummy's last club the Rabbit wondered: was his spade good? He had seen some very big spades discarded, but one could not trust people about such things. No, one could not be sure. Pity. It would be so nice to make the contract after all those rude remarks.

On dummy's last trump Papa had to throw a diamond to keep the ace of hearts. The Rabbit, feeling sure that the ace was still out, parted with his knave of hearts and Karapet let go a diamond to keep his spade. R.R. came to his hand with the king of diamonds and screwed his eyes while he searched his memory for stray spades.

He badly wanted to play the eight and twice he detached the card from his hand. What held him back was the thought that, if by some ugly chance, a higher spade was still out, he might not even make the ace of diamonds. And what would the Hog say then? It was too horrible to contemplate, so abandoning the idea reluctantly, he led a diamond to dummy's ace, remarking resignedly: "All right, you can have the last diamond."

But as the two was the only diamond out, the Rabbit himself could not contrive to lose it and the contract was duly made.

Fully restored to good-humour, the Hog jeered pleasantly: "I should have redoubled, of course. What stopped me was the thought that it might be interpreted as a Kock-Werner S.O.S. Bad luck, Papa. You did your best, but it just wasn't up to R.R.'s worst. Ha! Ha!"

Vive le Roi

A few days later, with H.H. and R.R. as their nearest rivals, Papa and Karapet were on the way to winning a big pairs event at the Unicorn. Two boards robbed them of victory. On the first a subtle defence by the Hog brought him a cold top. On the second too subtle a defence by Papa resulted in a near bottom.

This was the first of the fateful deals which, between them, tilted the balance:

North/South Game. Dealer West.

```
                 N
            W         E        ♠  A764
                 S             ♥  AQJ10
                               ◊  98
         ♠  KQ1092             ♣  A54
         ♥  K85
         ◊  Q105
         ♣  76
```

West	North	East	South
S.B.	*R.R.*	*Ch.Ch.*	*H.H.*
1◊	Pass	1♠	Pass
2◊	Pass	3♥	Pass
3NT	All Pass		

In an uncontested auction the Professor of Bio-Sophistry and Charlie the Chimp sailed into three no-trumps. The Rabbit opened the queen of clubs, won by the king in the closed hand. A heart followed. When the ten of hearts held, S.B. returned to his hand with the ace of diamonds to repeat the finesse. Again it succeeded, the Hog nonchalantly unguarding his king. Coming back with a diamond to the king the Secretary Bird finessed for the third time – and hissed viciously as the Hog pounced on dummy's queen of hearts with his king, cashed the queen of diamonds and exited with a club. The contract could no longer be made. This was the deal in full:

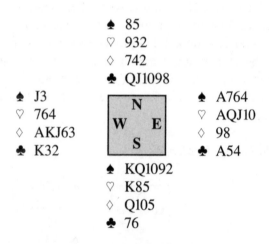

```
              ♠ 85
              ♡ 932
              ◊ 742
              ♣ QJ1098
♠ J3                        ♠ A764
♡ 764         N             ♡ AQJ10
◊ AKJ63     W   E           ◊ 98
♣ K32         S             ♣ A54
              ♠ KQ1092
              ♡ K85
              ◊ Q105
              ♣ 76
```

"One down?" said the Chimp incredulously, scanning the travelling scoresheet. "At every other table the contract was made. What went wrong?"

"Just this, that you had the ill-luck to be pitted against me," replied the Hog, casting down his eyes modestly. No one spoke. "Very well, then," he went on, "since you are all so curious to know, I had better explain my defence."

"For the barest opening," continued the Hideous Hog, "declarer had to have five diamonds, if not six, headed by the ace-king-knave. Since the queen was on the right side, he was predestined to make his contract. How could I deflect destiny's course? Only by outbidding her, that is, by offering declarer something better.

"If I could persuade him to accept my guarantee for the heart finesse, he would not need the finesse in diamonds for he could get home with four hearts, two top diamonds, two top clubs and the ace of spades. And in hearts, mind you, the finesse alone would suffice. In diamonds, unless he had six, he would need a 3-3 break as well.

"But, of course," went on the Hog, "I could not admit to the king of hearts until declarer had used up the entries to his hand, all three of them. Baring the king looked risky to the kibitzers, but I had nothing to lose, really, for the contract was otherwise doomed to succeed. It was what I call a black eye-to-nothing coup. Either I don't lose or opponents get a black eye."

Find the Lady
In the last round H.H. and R.R. met Walter the Walrus and Timothy the Toucan. This was the crucial deal:

Love All. Dealer South.

T.T.
- ♠ Q87
- ♡ A1072
- ◇ KQ10
- ♣ AJ10

R.R.
- ♠ J102
- ♡ J983
- ◇ J876
- ♣ 65

```
    N
W       E
    S
```

H.H.
- ♠ AK93
- ♡ 54
- ◇ 5432
- ♣ Q32

W.W.
- ♠ 654
- ♡ KQ6
- ◇ A9
- ♣ K9874

South	West	North	East
1NT	Pass	3NT	All Pass

The Rabbit opened the knave of spades which held the trick. Then came the ten of spades, covered by the queen in dummy and won by the Hog's king. The ace of spades followed, but concealing the nine of spades, the Hog switched to the three of diamonds.

The Walrus tried the hearts, but when H.H. threw the two of diamonds on the third round he was forced to look to the clubs for his ninth trick. Expecting R.R. to have the thirteenth spade, the Walrus took the club finesse against him.

"Surprise, surprise," chanted the Hog, as coming in with the queen of clubs he flicked the nine of spades across the table. The Walrus had fallen for an old ruse. A kibitzer gave him a pitying look.

I followed the board to Papa's table. A big hearty man with an orchid buttonhole was drinking champagne in the South seat. "Who's that?" I asked the Penguin who had come with me.

"That's Jeremy Joybell," said P.P. "He's the export manager of IMI, International Morticians Inc. The champagne is on expense account, of course. His partner is Lord Mortsbury, IMI's president."

Like the Walrus, J.J. became declarer in three no-trumps and like the Rabbit, Karapet opened the knave of spades. It held the trick. Papa, who was East, won the next two tricks with the king and ace. Again, like the Hog, the Greek cleverly concealed his last spade, playing at trick four the two of diamonds.

"Exactly the same sequence," observed Peregrine the Penguin.

J.J. tried the hearts. When they failed to break, he went into a short huddle. Emerging, he led the ace of clubs, then the knave, Papa played low and declarer ran it, raising an eyebrow when the Armenian followed suit.

The Greek threw his hands in the air with a gesture of despair. "What made you take this unnatural finesse?" he cried, more in anger than in sorrow. "You could not know that I had the last spade. How, then, could you, master player 1017, play so badly?"

Jeremy Joybell looked abashed. "You took me in completely," he confessed. "Of course, I assumed that your partner had the last spade, so I placed you with three spades, two hearts and presumably four diamonds. You led the two and it seemed unlikely that you would choose a false card in this situation. That left you with four clubs, so that when the queen did not come down on the first round, it meant that you simply had to have it. Yes, I am afraid you bamboozled me badly with your defence."

Peregrine turned to the Hog, who had finished his last set of boards and had come up to jeer at Papa.

"Is that why you carefully selected the three of diamonds and then discarded the two, suggesting a five-card suit?" asked the Penguin, "so that Walter should have no clue to your distribution?"

"Bah! That Walrus has no clue to anything anyway," retorted H.H. "But it's a matter of self-respect to play correctly even when one's alone."

We could hear Papa bemoaning his bottoms at the next table.

"Mind you," conceded the Hog grudgingly, "he was unlucky on that last board, for he played well up to a point. It was just that he struck one of the few players in the room good enough to miscount his hand. And, once again, he tried to be too clever. That two of diamonds was too subtle. Since he never plays true cards, no one who knew him would place him with a four-card suit. Unfortunately for Papa that undertaker fellow doesn't play here often enough to be familiar with his habits. Hence his bad luck."

Karapet Comes into his Own

"Bad luck? Papa's?" Karapet, who had overheard the Hog's last remark, was up in arms. "Papa doesn't come into it. It was my bad luck entirely, not his at all.

"You don't know the meaning of bad luck, my friends, the quality of bad luck. You need shed no tears for Papa. While he was dummy, for once, with no chance of outwitting himself, this was one of our boards:

♠ 1062
♡ A1032
◇ 8
♣ J10987

♠ KQJ
♡ KQJ
◇ KJ1097
♣ AK

West	North	East	South
1♠	Pass	Pass	Dble
Pass	2♣	Pass	3NT
All Pass			

West leads the five of spades, East following with the eight of spades. You win and lay down the ace-king of clubs. All follow, but there's no sign of the queen. You continue with the king-queen-knave of hearts and again all follow. I now invite you," went on the Armenian with a sardonic smile, "to make certain of your contract against any possible distribution of the outstanding cards."

The Hog raised a supercilious eyebrow and walked away. His own successes were so much more amusing than Karapet's misfortunes. The Owl was the first to speak. "We can set up the clubs," he began, "but having no second entry to the table we couldn't get back to enjoy them, and if we go for the diamonds, West will be a move ahead in clearing his spades. Very awkward."

"Are you saying that the contract can be made regardless of who has what?" asked the Penguin. "If West has the queen of clubs and the ace-queen of diamonds and at least five spades ..."

"Immaterial," rejoined the Armenian, cutting him short.

The Owl hooted. The Penguin puffed.

"I'd better tell you," went on Karapet, "for you don't look like getting there by yourselves. I overtook the knave of hearts with dummy's ace of hearts and threw my queen of spades on the ten of hearts. Next I led the knave of clubs and jettisoned the knave of spades. Now, if West cleared his spades, dummy's ten of spades would provide an entry to the clubs. If he cashed the ace of spades and exited with a diamond, I'd have plenty of time to set up my diamonds. Either way, I would have nine tricks."

"And is that what happened?" asked P.P. suspiciously.

"Precisely," replied Karapet.

"A very pretty solution to what looked like an insoluble problem and I congratulate you, Karapet, but where does your proverbial bad luck come into it?"

"The pretty solution to the insoluble problem didn't even get us an average!" replied the Armenian bitterly. "That's where bad luck comes in. The whole field was in three no-trumps. Every South made it, while one or two made ten tricks. It so happens that there exists no way of not solving the insoluble problem. There!" he added, filling in the other hands.

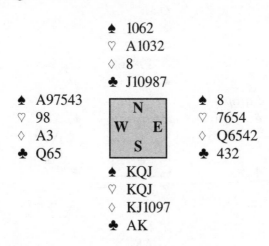

```
              ♠ 1062
              ♥ A1032
              ◇ 8
              ♣ J10987
♠ A97543       ┌─────────┐      ♠ 8
♥ 98           │    N    │      ♥ 7654
◇ A3           │ W     E │      ◇ Q6542
♣ Q65          │    S    │      ♣ 432
               └─────────┘
              ♠ KQJ
              ♥ KQJ
              ◇ KJ1097
              ♣ AK
```

We studied the diagram.

"Some Souths," went on Karapet, "took the finesse against the queen of diamonds and it worked, of course. One or two, more cunning than most, led a low diamond at trick two, hoping to slip past West's ace-queen. East won, but having no spade, he could do no damage. A couple of Wests failed to cash the queen of clubs while they had the chance. Hence our below average score."

We sympathised. Karapet looked up eagerly.

Karapet Retains Control

"Did I tell you what happened to me on Wednesday?" he began.

"Yes, of course," the Owl assured him hastily.

"Yes, indeed," echoed the Penguin apprehensively.

We had long ago developed a technique for not hearing Karapet's hard-luck stories, but this time we were clearly outmanoeuvred. Firmly barring the way to the door, he could pour out his troubles from a position of strength.

"I thought that you would like to hear about it," pursued Karapet. "There you are."

Game All. Dealer South.

O.M.
♠ -
♡ 5432
◇ J98765
♣ 1032

Karapet
♠ KQ1054
♡ 10876
◇ 32
♣ 85

```
      N
  W       E
      S
```

Papa
♠ A872
♡ AQ9
◇ Q104
♣ 976

R.R.
♠ J963
♡ KJ
◇ AK
♣ AKQJ4

"Against four hearts you make the obvious lead of the king of spades and ..."

"Did you say four hearts?" broke in the Penguin, and seeing the Armenian nod, he pressed the point. "How did South come to find himself in so improbable a contract?"

"Because," replied Karapet, "south was that crazy Rabbit. He was playing Flint and his partner wasn't."

I had kibitzed the rubber and remembered vividly how it all started. The Rabbit had cut a visitor from Outer Mongolia with an unpronounceable name, who asked to be addressed as "Yo".

"What shall we play?" he had enquired.

"Everything," replied the Rabbit enthusiastically. "Gerber, Stayman, Namyats ..."

"Blackwood?" enquired Yo.

"Of course agreed R.R., "and Texas, Fishbein, Flint ..."

Wishing no doubt that he was back safely in Ulan Bator, the Outer Mongolian agreed quickly, before worse befell him. His English wasn't nearly good enough to engage in argument. This was the bidding sequence:

South	West	North	East
2NT	Pass	3◊	Pass
3♡	Pass	4♡	All Pass

Yo wasn't sure whether two no-trumps was or wasn't forcing and it didn't dawn on him that three diamonds could be treated as conventional, calling for an automatic response of three hearts. He was much relieved to hear partner bid hearts – it could so easily have been spades and he was only too glad to raise him.

The Rabbit ruffed the king of spades in dummy, came to hand with the ace of diamonds and ruffed another. After cashing the king of diamonds and the ace-king of clubs, he ruffed a third spade, then a diamond with his knave of hearts. With five cards left he ruffed his last spade, leaving this end-position.

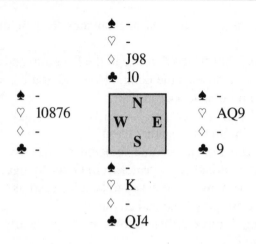

```
              ♠ -
              ♡ -
              ◇ J98
              ♣ 10

   ♠ -            N            ♠ -
   ♡ 10876    W      E        ♡ AQ9
   ◇ -                        ◇ -
   ♣ -            S            ♣ 9

              ♠ -
              ♡ K
              ◇ -
              ♣ QJ4
```

A diamond from dummy now allowed the king of hearts to score the tenth trick *en passant*.

"You will observe," said the Armenian, "that after the natural spade opening the four hearts extravaganza is unbeatable while three no trumps is two down from the start, not that any sane pair would bid game, anyway."

Karapet sat back in an ecstasy of anguish. To paraphrase Lord Acton, it isn't enough to be unlucky, one must be seen to be unlucky, and not for many years had he held a captive audience long enough to tell them all the gory details of two of his choicest catastrophies.

Chapter Eight
Papa's Turn

Colin the Corgi, the facetious young Griffin from Oxbridge, was in melancholy mood. "Our friend, Papa," he said with a mirthless smile, "firmly believes that it is better to be too clever and lose than not to be clever at all."

"He let you down?" asked the Owl sympathetically.

Colin's look dismissed this as a gross understatement. "Papa is enjoying a good run," he said bitterly. "Just as at times you get a spate of slams or freak distributions, so lately the furies have conjured up a succession of deals to bring out the worst in him. And that tortuous mind needs so little encouragement. Let one devious ploy come off and he will stoop at nothing straightforward for the rest of the session."

As he spoke, Colin wrote down a hand and, covering up the East/West holdings, he invited us to make four spades.

```
        ♠ 87
        ♡ QJ102
        ◇ AKJ9
        ♣ 432
```

```
        N
    W       E
        S
```

```
        ♠ AKJ1064
        ♡ A6
        ◇ 432
        ♣ 107
```

South	West	North	East
1♠	2♣	2◇	Pass
2♠	Pass	3♠	Pass
4♠	All Pass		

"West starts with the three top clubs. East follows and you ruff. Carry on." Colin sat back with a satirical expression which implied, "Whatever you do, you'll wish you had done something else."

Oscar the Owl, our Senior Kibitzer, blinked cautiously.

Peregrine the Penguin, his opposite number at the Unicorn, concurred gravely.

Timothy the Toucan was the first to speak. "We've lost two tricks already and we may lose a heart or a diamond. We must, therefore, seek the best chance of not losing a spade as well. So, a diamond to the king and ..."

"No, no," interrupted Walter the Walrus. "You are neglecting a safety play. First you must lay down the ace of spades, in case West has the singleton queen, then ..."

C.C. broke in with a contemptuous gurgle. When it subsided, O.O. explained: "If West has a singleton spade, East has four and he is therefore four times as likely as West to have the queen of spades. So, since you may have to repeat the finesse, you cannot afford to lay down the ace."

With an imperious jerk of his short flipper-like arms, the Penguin called for silence: "That's settled. We cross to dummy with a diamond and take the finesse in trumps. What happens?"

The Corgi told him. "West follows with the seven of diamonds and East with the six of diamonds. East's trump is the two and West's the nine. Proceed."

The Owl hooted softly. "Just shows you how wrong it would have been to play that ace of spades," he said, turning to the Walrus. "Unless the nine of spades is a false card, East's holding is ♠ Q532, so we must finesse again. Another diamond then, this time taking the finesse ..."

"It wins – West plays the eight of diamonds, East plays the five," interjected C.C.

"... and a trump to our knave," concluded O.O.

"This time, West wins with the queen of spades and gives partner a diamond ruff for the fourth, setting trick," said Colin, showing us the complete deal:

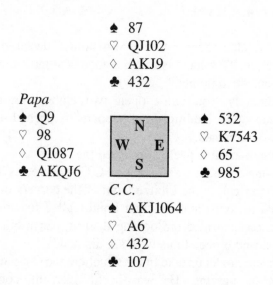

```
                    ♠ 87
                    ♡ QJ102
                    ◊ AKJ9
                    ♣ 432
        Papa
        ♠ Q9          ┌─────────┐      ♠ 532
        ♡ 98          │    N    │      ♡ K7543
        ◊ Q1087       │  W   E  │      ◊ 65
        ♣ AKQJ6       │    S    │      ♣ 985
                      └─────────┘
                    C.C.
                    ♠ AKJ1064
                    ♡ A6
                    ◊ 432
                    ♣ 107
```

"That's how I played it, I fear," went on the Corgi, "and I won't deny that, for once, Papa's cunning paid handsomely for he succeeded in breaking an unbreakable contract. He could see that any finesse I might need would be right, so he had no qualms about risking his queen of spades, not after East's six of diamonds had pointed the way to a clever defence. Being the highest diamond out it almost certainly showed a doubleton, so Papa had a lot to gain and nothing to lose by holding up that queen of trumps."

"Didn't I tell you," broke in the Walrus triumphantly, "that you should have laid down the ace of spades. Had you done that no one could have bamboozled you."

We were too busy examining the next hand to spare W.W. the usual withering look.

A Remarkable Pack

"It's nice to hold a powerhouse for a change," went on the Corgi, "so I present you with this little lot."

♠ A K Q J   ♡ A 7 2   ◇ A 4   ♣ A 5 3 2

"I prefer a two club opening to two no-trumps," declared P.P. after due deliberation. "The hand is worth a good deal more than its face value of twenty-two points."

"Unfortunately, you can't open two clubs," replied C.C., looking smug. "The bidding, it so happens, is opened in front of you with two diamonds."

"A truly remarkable pack," observed the Owl.

"Papa, whose hand it was," went on C.C., "purred as he passed, watching the effect on the kibitzers out of the corners of his eyes. North raised to four diamonds and South called four no-trumps. While Papa concentrated on looking distrait, North bid six clubs and South closed proceedings with six diamonds."

After pausing to let us take in the situation, the Corgi continued: "Papa kept on passing. He was in his element, cool, clever, unpredictable. No one else would think of passing on such a hand, but then Papa had no wish to be like anyone else.

"The ace of trumps is the book lead in such cases and Papa, for
once, agreed with the book. And now, my friends, comes the
crucial question: Having taken a good look at dummy, what do you
lead at trick two?"

♠ 108765
♡ KQJ3
◇ 8765
♣ -

♠ AKQJ
♡ A72
◇ A4
♣ A532

	N	
W		E
	S	

"The ace of spades, of course," spluttered the Walrus. "Even if
declarer ruffs, it can't hurt."

"Another trump, I should have thought," ventured O.O.

"It's the logical continuation," agreed P.P.

Colin the Corgi shook his head. "Either play might cost the
contract," he warned. "Try to picture declarer's hand. Where's his
two-bid? Apart from diamonds, his high cards can only be in clubs.
So he has good clubs missing the ace. He applied Blackwood, so he
may have a singleton in one of the majors. But either way,
everything hinges on the clubs and declarer can hardly go wrong.
Inevitably, he will play Papa for the ace of clubs, set up his clubs
and discard from dummy the suit in which he has a singleton. Does
that suggest a defence?"

The Owl looked inscrutable. The Penguin and the Toucan
looked at the Owl.

"To give declarer an alternative line of play, one that might fail,"
pursued C.C., "Papa underled his ace of clubs. A very ingenious
move, you must admit, and now you see why it would have been so
unwise to lead a second trump. If declarer has enough clubs, six or
maybe even seven, he might hope to bring down East's ace by
ruffing three times in dummy. But the prospect of two ruffs would
hardly tempt him. Note also how much Papa had improved his

chances by concealing his powerhouse. Since he passed throughout, there was nothing to suggest that he was more likely than East to have the ace of clubs."

"Did Papa really lead a small club?" asked the Toucan incredulously.

"And declarer ruffed, hoping to bring down East's ace?" The Walrus sounded equally unbelieving.

"Yes, to both questions," replied the Corgi. "Declarer ruffed, returned to the closed hand by trumping a spade, ruffed a second club, came back with another spade ruff, paused, thought things over – and proceeded to fulfil his contract," added C.C., amid a chorus of raised eyebrows.

We looked at the complete deal:

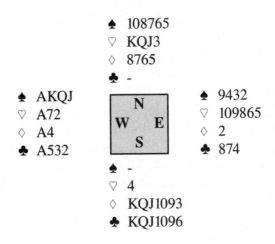

```
                    ♠  108765
                    ♡  KQJ3
                    ◇  8765
                    ♣  -
      ♠  AKQJ                       ♠  9432
      ♡  A72          N             ♡  109865
      ◇  A4        W     E          ◇  2
      ♣  A532         S             ♣  874
                    ♠  -
                    ♡  4
                    ◇  KQJ1093
                    ♣  KQJ1096
```

"With dummy's last trump still very much in being," went on C.C., "South ran the king of clubs, then, on the next round, he caught Papa's ace."

"What made him change horses in mid-stream?" asked the Penguin.

"Yes," echoed the Owl, "if at first he thought that the ace of clubs was with East, why should he suddenly decide to play West for it?"

"Because," replied the Corgi, "Papa couldn't leave well alone.

Having found a clever lead to beat the contract, he had to be too clever and beat himself. In underleading the ace of clubs, he selected the subtle three of clubs. Next time, he completed the deception by following delicately with the two.

"Now declarer was a simple soul who played down the middle and believed what he was told. Since Papa's three-two sequence indicated a five-card suit, his partner could have only a doubleton. So when the ace of clubs failed to come down in two rounds, he grit his teeth and played Papa for it. That poor Papa," added the Corgi bitterly, "he's so busy fooling all the people all the time that he won't take pity even on himself. It's pretty hard on his partner, just the same."

"Not like you to be sorry for a mere partner," interposed the Walrus. No one had ever caught C.C. being sorry for anyone before.

"*I* was Papa's mere partner," snapped back the Corgi.

Papa's Petard

Another hand, which Fate must have intended especially for Papa's benefit, came up a little later that same afternoon. I watched it sitting behind the Greek, who had Colin once more as his partner. His traditional enemy, the Hideous Hog, was his right-hand opponent. These were the North/South hands:

♠ 976
♡ Q3
◊ AQJ8643
♣ K

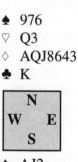

♠ AJ2
♡ A85
◊ 92
♣ AQ1085

South	West	North	East
Papa	*S.S.*	*C.C.*	*H.H.*
		1◇	Pass
2♣	Pass	2◇	Pass
3NT	All Pass		

West, the straight-down-the-middle Simple Soul, who had been South on the previous deal, opened the king of spades and Papa counted his tricks. In a pairs event, he wouldn't have settled for less than twelve for it only needed the diamond finesse. A little luck with the clubs as well and all thirteen tricks would be in the bag.

Since he was only in three no-trumps, however, Papa's sole concern was to ensure the contract against bad distribution and more especially against finding East with the king of diamonds. Was any watertight safety play available? And what precisely should he do at trick one? If he played the two on the king of spades, West would doubtless switch to a heart and that could prove fatal. If he won the first trick with the ace of spades, and H.H. turned up with the king of diamonds, a second spade through his knave-two could be just as lethal.

Suddenly, something flashed through Papa's mind. Just in time he remembered a striking hand which he had seen in a book. The situation was similar to the one now confronting him and declarer had solved his problem by bringing off a breathtaking coup, a play worthy of Papa himself.

Following the model in his mind's eye, Papa threw the knave of spades on the king! Of course, West, as intended, led another spade. The Greek looked round for applause, for his troubles, he felt, were almost over. If the vital diamond finesse failed and the Hog led another spade, the suit would have broken harmlessly. And if West had started with five spades, the Hog would not have one to play.

At trick three, Papa led the nine of diamonds and finessed. The knave held. H.H. dropped the ten and all was well – so far. There was still the risk that his ten was a false card and that he was holding up the king. Coming back to his hand by overtaking the king of clubs with the ace, Papa finessed again. As he led his two of diamonds he had a contingency plan all ready. If West showed out, he would go up with the ace of diamonds and play another to the Hog's king. So long as H.H. had the king of hearts, there would still be a good chance to bring home the contract. West, however, followed to the second round of diamonds and Papa heaved a sigh of relief. He was still heaving when the Hog covered dummy's queen with the king and shot a heart through the closed hand. These were the four hands:

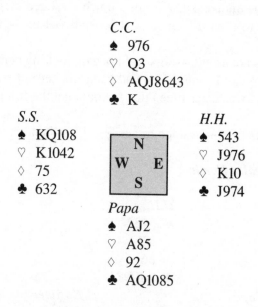

C.C.
♠ 976
♡ Q3
◇ AQJ8643
♣ K

S.S.
♠ KQ108
♡ K1042
◇ 75
♣ 632

H.H.
♠ 543
♡ J976
◇ K10
♣ J974

Papa
♠ AJ2
♡ A85
◇ 92
♣ AQ1085

"I suppose you realise, Themistocles," jeered the Hideous Hog, "that nothing but that shattering piece of deception with the knave of spades could have lost you the contract. The spades break. The diamonds break. The king of hearts is where you want it. Every card is right and there is no way of beating you – unless you do it yourself, of course."

"Daring play, holding up the king of diamonds," observed a kibitzer admiringly. "I don't know anyone else who'd have the nerve to do it."

"Daring?" cried the Greek indignantly. "Why, he learned it

from me. He saw me do it less than hour ago when I was defending a four spades contract against Colin and now you give *him* credit for *my* play!"

"And so, you see," concluded Colin the Corgi sadly, after describing the hand. "Once more I was hoist on his petard."

Too Clever by Half

A few days after this conversation I ran into Papa at the bar. "What a pity that you didn't stay to see that last hand before dinner," he began, with the unmistakable air of a much-wronged man. All the signs pointed to a hard-luck story. I looked hastily for a way of escape.

"Surely it's not as late as this ..." I began, looking at my watch. The Greek was not listening. He had been the hero of some great misfortune and was determined that I should get the full benefit of it.

On the back of an envelope he scribbled this hand.

Game All. Dealer North.

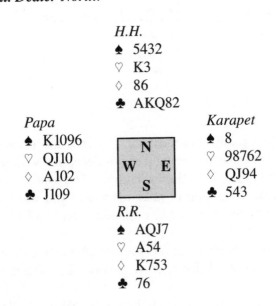

```
                    H.H.
                    ♠ 5432
                    ♡ K3
                    ◇ 86
                    ♣ AKQ82
   Papa                              Karapet
   ♠ K1096          ┌─────────┐      ♠ 8
   ♡ QJ10           │    N    │      ♡ 98762
   ◇ A102           │  W   E  │      ◇ QJ94
   ♣ J109           │    S    │      ♣ 543
                    └─────────┘
                    R.R.
                    ♠ AQJ7
                    ♡ A54
                    ◇ K753
                    ♣ 76
```

South	West	North	East
		1♣	Pass
1♠	Pass	2♠	Pass
3◊	Pass	3♠	Pass
3NT	All Pass		

This was Papa's story. "I led the queen of hearts which held, Karapet signalling with the nine. Dummy's king of hearts won the next trick and the Rabbit led a spade. Karapet produced the eight and I took the queen with the king. Well, what do you do next?"

I considered the prospects to be unfavourable and said so.

"Unfavourable? You mean hopeless, of course," cried the Greek. "The contract is foolproof. In fact, it's Rabbit-proof."

Adroitly flicking his long, hairy fingers, he peeled off declarer's tricks: "Five clubs, yes? Ace and king of hearts, yes? And he bid a spade, remember. So he must have the ace and knave left. Nine, solid, indestructible tricks."

Papa lit a second gold-tipped cigarette and challenged me: "How do you set out to beat this unbeatable contract?"

"Any hope," I ventured, "that Karapet will produce the king and queen of diamonds?"

"None."

"Or that he will suddenly discover the ace of hearts?"

"No, no, don't try anything far-fetched. And forget for the moment that declarer is our friend the Rabbit. Imagine that it's the Hog or any other good player. What do you do?"

I could think of nothing on the spur of the moment.

"The answer," declared Papa triumphantly, "is to lead a club!" Unable to follow, I tried to look superior.

"Consider," went on the Greek. "Scratch under the surface. You know two things which declarer cannot know. He expects the spades to break three-two and to yield him three tricks. You know that they won't.

"But he does not know, and you do, that against the odds, the clubs will produce all five tricks, if he needs them. Yes?"

I agreed.

"Therefore," continued Papa, "reckoning on three tricks in spades, declarer will seek to ensure four more in clubs for his contract – not three or five, mark you, but precisely four. And as he can have no more than two clubs himself – we know of eleven other cards in his hand he must duck a club once. Yes?"

It was true.

"But I had to hurry," pursued Papa. "Once declarer found out that the spades were four-one he would need all five clubs. He could no longer afford to duck, especially if I cleared the hearts, and I would miss my chance of stealing the decisive trick."

"So you led a club?" I asked.

"Certainly," replied Papa, "and had the Hog found that defence he would have been lauded to the skies. It would have been recognised by all as a masterstroke. As it was, no one even noticed it," he observed bitterly.

"At least," I said, "you had the satisfaction of breaking a Rabbit-proof contract."

Papa shook his head. "What's the use of a masterstroke against the Rabbit? Casting pearls before swine! He just cashed his clubs without knowing what he was doing."

"Hard on you," I said, trying to sound sympathetic, "but one can hardly expect R.R. to spot every safety play and anyway he probably miscounted his tricks. Next time you devise a masterstroke," I added, "you must find an opponent worthy of it."

Karapet, joining us, registered dissent with both black eyebrows.

"Don't malign the poor Rabbit," he said. "It is not because he is simple that he made his contract. It is solely because Papa is so clever. What club do you suppose he led?"

"How could that matter?" exclaimed the Greek.

"He chose the ten from knave-ten-nine," went on the Armenian, "such a clever card! He wanted to deceive and he succeeded – with a vengeance. "The Rabbit was too frightened to duck. He thought that I would overtake the ten with the knave and shoot through a diamond, the last thing he wanted. Oh yes, he admitted it." And turning with a sad look to Papa, the Armenian added: "What's the use of being so clever when you cannot help outwitting yourself?"

Chapter Nine
From Austerlitz to Waterloo

Undaunted by his misfortunes, Papa was in a belligerent mood when we met the next day in the card room. "Learn to fight back," he declared, waving his arms as we sat chatting, waiting for the game to start.

The gesture was eloquent of his exasperation with the Hideous Hog, who had been getting away with mass murder and reviling his victims into the bargain for defending themselves so feebly.

"He mesmerises the lot of you," went on the Greek, looking the Rueful Rabbit straight between the ears. Timothy the Toucan bounced uneasily in his armchair, his long crimson nose reflecting a sense of guilt. Even Oscar the Owl, our Senior Kibitzer, looked uncomfortable as if he, too, came under the indictment. Only Walter the Walrus remained unperturbed. After all, Papa could hardly have *him* in mind, and he had always suspected the others of playing out of their class.

"First you are too craven to double," pursued Papa indignantly, "then you allow him to make unmakable contracts."

"But you can't have it both ways, Papa," protested O.O. "If he's going to make his unmakable contract, it surely can't be right to double."

"Empty excuses," replied Papa contemptuously. "Stand up to him. Don't be afraid. Don't be flustered. Do as I do and ... why, talk of the devil ..."

Papa broke off as H.H. himself appeared through the doorway. "No, thank you," he said, accepting one of Oscar's Havanas and putting it away carefully in his capacious cigar-case. "I smoke too much as it is." A minute later, he had cut the Rabbit against Papa and the Walrus. Sitting between the Greek and R.R., this is what I could see.

Love All. Dealer South.

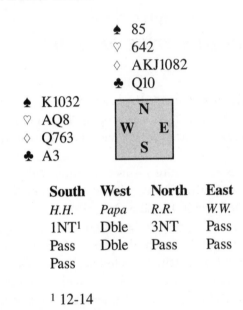

♠ 85
♡ 642
◇ AKJ1082
♣ Q10

♠ K1032
♡ AQ8
◇ Q763
♣ A3

South	West	North	East
H.H.	*Papa*	*R.R.*	*W.W.*
1NT[1]	Dble	3NT	Pass
Pass	Dble	Pass	Pass
Pass			

[1] 12-14

"No such bidding," said Papa severely, as the Rabbit tabled his hand.

The three of spades, the nearest false card to his thumb, was the Greek's opening lead. The Walrus produced the queen and the Hog won the trick with the ace. A club to dummy's queen came next, and when Papa played low, H.H. continued with a second club to the ace, W.W. contributing the six and seven. Gathering the trick, the Greek gave dummy the sort of look which Napoleon must have cast over the field of battle at Austerlitz. Victory was in the air and well he knew it. First he cashed the king of spades. Then, when only red cards remained on the table, he swished the queen of diamonds triumphantly into the jaws of dummy's powerful diamond suit.

Auto-Squeeze

The Hog paused. As second followed second, Papa beamed. "Take your time," he said with quiet condescension. "Not that it will help you very much." Clearing his throat, he summed up the situation.

"If you have three diamonds, you can't lose. Obviously you haven't or you wouldn't be thinking. You can't have a singleton for you opened one no-trump. So, you have a doubleton. Well, you can take your six diamonds, but you will find, I fear, that the last one will squeeze you inexorably. Yes, you will be the victim of a self-inflicted auto-squeeze. First cousin to the suicide squeeze. Ha! Ha! Dummy will be down to three cards, all hearts. And what, pray, will you have? If you throw the knave of spades – with which you are marked, since W.W. played the queen – I will keep my spades and the ace of hearts. And if you retain the knave, I will throw my spades away, keeping three unbeatable hearts. For you will be discarding before me, don't forget.

"Of course," Papa went on, glowing with admiration for Papa, "one of your two diamonds may be the nine, and if so, you can win the second diamond trick in your hand. But then, if dummy contributes two diamond tricks only, you won't make nine, will you? Or rather I will win five, for before you can set up a heart, I can set up a spade and ..."

The Greek had plenty more to say but the Hog cut him short by covering the queen of diamonds with the king and continuing with the ace and knave. The Walrus followed once, then he threw the six and seven of spades – to give partner the count, as he explained later. On the third round the Hog discarded the seven of hearts.

The Greek was still wearing the Austerlitz look when H.H., switching suddenly from one end of the diamond suit to the other, picked the two. From his hand he threw the knave of hearts and Papa, much to his surprise, found himself capturing a trick with his last baby diamond. Walter the Walrus contributed the five of clubs, a delayed echo, but by now no one had much time for him.

This was the five-card end-position:

```
          ♠  -
          ♡  642
          ◇  108
          ♣  -
♠ 102
♡ AQ8
◇ -
♣ -
```

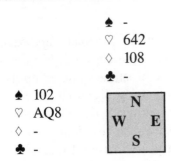

"So," said Papa, "he thinks he is playing with children! Am I really supposed to fall for that knave of hearts, H.H., and to imagine that you have kindly bared your king for my benefit? Let me tell you, then, your last five cards, in case you don't know yourself! Your shape was, of course, 3-4-2-4. And now," went on Papa, "since you apparently don't want to squeeze yourself, I will endplay you instead. So!" Flicking the two of spades on the table, Papa waited for the applause.

"Conceding the last trick," said the Hog with a good-natured sneer, as he exposed his hand.

The full deal was:

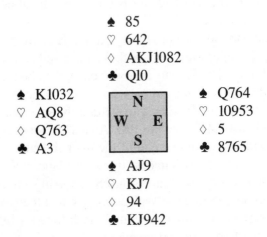

```
              ♠ 85
              ♡ 642
              ◇ AKJ1082
              ♣ Q10
♠ K1032                    ♠ Q764
♡ AQ8                      ♡ 10953
◇ Q763                     ◇ 5
♣ A3                       ♣ 8765
              ♠ AJ9
              ♡ KJ7
              ◇ 94
              ♣ KJ942
```

"I congratulate you, Papa, on a new coup," said the Hog with mock solemnity. "What was the name you gave it? Auto-squeeze?

Shouldn't it be Auto-deception or would you prefer Phantom Endplay?"

"Why didn't you signal in clubs to show four?" cried Papa.

"I did," snorted the Walrus, "but you were too inebriated by your own eloquence to notice it. All I had was my usual two points and you blame me for throwing the contract!"

Textbook Situation

The Hideous Hog was still jeering happily at the Greek when this hand came up.

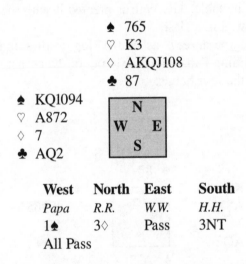

```
                    ♠ 765
                    ♡ K3
                    ◇ AKQJ108
                    ♣ 87
    ♠ KQ1094      ┌─────────┐
    ♡ A872        │    N    │
    ◇ 7           │  W   E  │
    ♣ AQ2         │    S    │
                  └─────────┘
```

West	North	East	South
Papa	*R.R.*	*W.W.*	*H.H.*
1♠	3◇	Pass	3NT
All Pass			

"I hope you won't be disappointed in my little lot," said the Rabbit apprehensively, as he tabled his hand, "but we didn't agree on whether jump overcalls should be forcing or pre-emptive, did we? So I can't be wrong both ways. I mean, if you don't know what to expect, you can't blame me for not having it, can you? I mean ..."

R.R. went on dithering amiably while Papa, whose king of spades held the first trick, considered the situation. The Walrus had followed with the two of spades and H.H. had played the three. Clearly he had the ace-knave left, and that meant that he had seven top tricks plus the king of hearts poised over the ace. He needed one more only for his contract, so the defence could take no risks.

At trick two, Papa switched to the two of hearts, a probing move, which could not cost a trick. The Hog played dummy's three and felled Walter's nine with his queen. Next he led the knave of hearts to Papa's ace, dummy's king and Walter's six.

What would be Papa's next move?

"A textbook situation," whispered Oscar, who was sitting on my left, next to dummy. "The Hog is obviously trying to set up his ten of hearts for the ninth trick. Unless Walter can produce the king of clubs there's no hope."

Before O.O. had completed the sentence, the ace of clubs was on the way to the table. The Walrus greeted it with the nine, and the queen followed in a flash.

"Eleven? Do you agree?" asked the Hog, totting up the rubber points and watching Papa maliciously out of the corner of his eye.

These were the four hands:

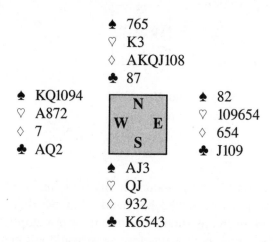

```
              ♠ 765
              ♡ K3
              ◊ AKQJ108
              ♣ 87
♠ KQ1094                      ♠ 82
♡ A872         N              ♡ 109654
◊ 7          W   E            ◊ 654
♣ AQ2          S              ♣ J109
              ♠ AJ3
              ♡ QJ
              ◊ 932
              ♣ K6543
```

"A pretty percentage play, don't you think?" asked the Hog, beaming at each of his opponents in turn.

"*What* did you call it?" asked the Walrus incredulously. "A percentage play?"

"But, of course, my dear Walter," the Hog assured him, "on my play it couldn't possibly dawn on Papa that I didn't have the ten of hearts, so ..."

"But he might have had it himself," protested W.W.

"Certainly," agreed H.H., "but on the bidding you were likely to be longer in hearts than Papa. So I had better than a fifty-fifty chance of finding you with the ten. That's why I called it a percentage play. What's more, the odds were distinctly attractive since I was unlikely to make nine tricks otherwise."

"Very lucky for all that," observed Oscar the Owl, shaking his head. "If Papa has the ten of hearts you can go four down."

"Don't you believe it," countered H.H. "I can never go more than one down for if Papa has the ten, the suit's blocked. Don't forget that he must have the eight too, since Walter played the nine on the first round."

Menacing noises could be heard coming from the back of Papa's throat, but they didn't add up to coherent speech.

"You know," went on the Hideous Hog, "I am not sure that even if Papa had the ten of hearts himself, he would have been so ready to believe it. For just as some players miss the simplest inferences and see nothing, so others have second sight and see everything, including things that aren't there. Nothing impersonal, of course," added H.H., sneering benignly at Papa.

The Greek ignored him. He seemed tired and dejected and there was nothing of the Austerlitz air about him as he told the steward, "Get me a taxi, Robin, I have a train to catch at Waterloo."

Thinking Like a Rattler

"You look pleased with yourself," I said to H.H., as we waited for the Bollinger when the session was over. "I suppose you don't often get the chance to bamboozle Papa twice in such quick succession."

The Hog didn't seem to hear me. There was a faraway look in his eyes. "I wonder," he mused, "who lent me that book. I've had it such a long time."

"What book?" I asked.

"One by Ossie and Jim Jacoby," replied H.H. "There's a story in it about the champion rattlesnake catcher in Texas or Mexico or New York, or somewhere like that. He was asked for the secret of his success and he said: 'To catch a rattler you have to think like a rattler.' Profound words. Think like your quarry, then you'll know which way he'll jump. Take Papa and those two hands he misdefended. I tried to think as he does. He would surely throw the knave of hearts ostentatiously, keeping a small one to make me think that he's bared his king. So he thought that I'd do the same. You can always trust a rattlesnake," concluded the Hog, "so long as you can think as he does."

Chapter Ten
Advance Retaliation

"I have made a mistake," said the Hideous Hog.

It seemed impossible, but his sepuchral tones left no doubt that he was speaking in earnest and we expressed our deepest sympathy.

"The second mistake in less than six years," went on H.H. lugubriously. "People will be saying that I am losing my touch."

"Six years?" echoed Oscar the Owl, our Senior Kibitzer. "I don't recall the occasion."

"11th June it was," said the Hog sombrely. "There had been an earthquake in Japan that week. Then, two days later, a hurricane struck Guadeloupe. A Wednesday it was and on the Friday I had a ridiculous lapse in endplaying the Rabbit. I am not really superstitious, you know, but these things always seem to happen in threes."

We made friendly noises. "So easy to mistime a throw-in," observed someone sympathetically.

"No excuse," snapped the Hog, "and I'm not asking for crocodile tears either. It was a childishly simply endplay. I stripped the hand, or so I thought, and I put him in with the last diamond, leaving him no choice but to return a club, giving me a ruff and discard, or to lead into my heart tenace. A classical endplay. But no, not against the Rabbit. He exited nonchalantly with a spade – from the other pack, of course."

"But surely," objected O.O., "that would have given him a card too many and someone would have spotted it."

"Not a bit of it," replied H.H. bitterly. "He had shed a club on the floor earlier on and it didn't come to light until it was too late. At the time, believe it or not, I thought that I'd miscounted the hand."

"And was that the trouble again today?" asked Oscar.

The Hideous Hog wasn't listening. He was too busy drawing the familiar diagram. As he filled in the North/South hands a low hissing sound proclaimed the approach of S.B., the Emeritus Professor of Bio-Sophistry.

"You are just in time, Professor," said H.H. by way of greeting. "Play my hand, sitting South. Papa is West and Walter the Walrus is his partner. I've got the Rabbit, as usual, but for once I am playing the hand, so he doesn't come into it.

Game All. Dealer North.

```
          ♠ 43
          ♡ KJ6
          ◇ KJ
          ♣ AKJ942
         ┌─────────┐
         │    N    │
         │ W     E │
         │    S    │
         └─────────┘
          ♠ J109
          ♡ A98
          ◇ A5432
          ♣ 83
```

South	West	North	East
H.H.	*Papa*	*R.R.*	*W.W.*
		1♣	Pass
1◇	Dble	Pass	1♠
Pass	Pass	3♣	Pass
3NT	All Pass		

"As you can see," went on the Hog, "the bidding is straight-forward and ..."

"I can't quite see your spade stopper," interrupted the Secretary Bird, registering a low derisory gurgle at the back of his throat.

"If you can make three no-trumps without one," retorted the Hog, "you don't require a spade stopper."

"The spades may break four-four," pointed out Oscar helpfully.

The Hog described the play to the first four tricks. "Papa opened the three top spades, the queen, the king, then the ace. The Walrus beckoned him on with the six, the five and the eight, in that order. At trick four Papa led the queen of clubs. Carry on, Professor." The Hog held out invitingly a fat, podgy hand.

The Emeritus Professor pondered, stroking his round chinless face. Then, thrusting long spidery fingers behind the lapels of his coat, he held forth in his most academic style.

"We repress the first unthinking impulse to cover the queen with the king and ask ourselves: if West had no more spades, why does he not switch to a red suit, hoping to find his partner with the ace? The answer, no doubt, is that West has both red queens himself and is loth to give declarer a free finesse. Neither does he expect on the bidding to find his partner with an ace. So we come to the next question: why does West lead the queen of clubs? Why not a low one? Yes, my friends, you have guessed correctly. The queen of clubs is bare and will come down anyway, but if declarer wins the trick, East's ten of clubs will provide an unexpected entry to the two long spades.

"And so, you see," concluded the Secretary Bird, untwining his long wiry legs, "we play low to the queen of clubs, allowing West to hold the trick. Now nothing can go wrong. Of course, if West has another club we have given away a trick, but we can afford to lose it if thereby we ensure the contract. That is the essence of every safety play."

The expression of utter misery on the Hog's face brought S.B. to a sudden halt. "You missed it?" asked S.B., with a look in which triumph was nicely blended with pity. "Console yourself, my friend, we all make mistakes. Why, only last year I ..."

"It's worse than I thought," gasped the Hideous Hog. "I knew that I blundered, but to think that I played the hand the same way as that, er, Professor. Yes, I, too, thought that Papa had no more spades and that he was trying to create an entry to Walter's hand. I played low and with a deafening jeer he cashed his fourth spade and now he will be gloating for weeks to come."

These were the four hands.

R.R.
♠ 43
♡ KJ6
◇ KJ
♣ AKJ942

Papa
♠ AKQ2
♡ Q1075
◇ Q109
♣ Q10

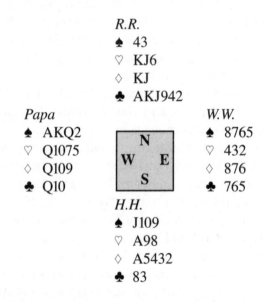

W.W.
♠ 8765
♡ 432
◇ 876
♣ 765

H.H.
♠ J109
♡ A98
◇ A5432
♣ 83

Oscar the Owl was the first to speak. "The Greek put up a very cunning defence, but you could hardly tell that he had another spade, so why should you reproach yourself?"

The Hog freshened his glass with the contents of the Professor's and clearing his throat, explained:

"If Papa had four black cards only, three spades and one club, he would have had a five-card suit, presumably hearts. With five hearts and three spades, would he have passed one spade, running the risk that the Walrus might play the hand? Of course not. Besides, don't we all know that Papa never passes without four-card support for his partner's suit?"

The Rabbit, who had followed attentively the Hog's analysis, sighed deeply. "I wish," he said ruefully, "that I could think these things out like you people do, but I am afraid that I will never play well enough to go down on a hand like that. I mean, you have to see so far ahead not to make nine tricks, that is ..."

The Hog Fights Back

With a fat, imperious forefinger, the Hog silenced him. "You may be sure," he declared, "that I didn't let him get away with it. I hit back immediately. Here is the hand. I held it against him on Wednesday."

"Wednesday?" repeated the Owl, with a puzzled expression. "But I thought that the hand you just showed us came up this afternoon. So how could you hit back before being hit, as it were?"

"Advance retaliation," explained H.H., "much the best kind, I assure you, especially against Themistocles. Anyway, here you are, sitting South. Papa, East, deals:

         ♠ A43
         ♡ QJ763
         ◇ J3
         ♣ QJ5

```
        N
    W       E
        S
```

         ♠ K107652
         ♡ AK4
         ◇ AK
         ♣ 32

South	West	North	East
			1◇
Dble	Pass	2♡	ass
3♠	Pass	4♠	Pass
4NT	Pass	5◇	Pass
6♣	Pass	6♠	All Pass

"I doubled Papa's opening bid of one diamond," pursued H.H., "and hearing two hearts from partner, I naturally visualised a slam."

"With two losing clubs?" sneered the Secretary Bird.

"With *no* losing clubs," replied the Hog firmly. "If a club isn't led, you needn't lose one, need you? Conversely, if there is any danger of a club lead, you don't have to bid a slam, do you? As I was about to tell you when you interrupted me, over partner's two hearts I bid three spades. I would have passed four hearts, of course, but fortunately, with a fit in spades, he raised me. Now it only remained for me to apply Blackwood to check on aces and the slam became an odds-on proposition."

"And what was that comic six club bid?" enquired the Emeritus Professor.

"Merely to confuse the issue, which is always a good thing," replied H.H., "and also annoy Papadopoulos which is even better. It must have made his hackles rise to hear me tell his partner that I had his ace of clubs. Ha! Ha!

"Anyway," pursued the Hideous Hog, "the Walrus opened the nine of diamonds to the knave, queen and ace. At trick two I led a trump and the Walrus produced the queen and ..."

"And you lived happily ever after," interjected S.B. contemptuously. "The trumps broke two-two, of course, so you made your horrible contract and gloated for the rest of the evening."

"It was the afternoon session," corrected the Hog angrily, "and I did not say how the trumps were split."

"The contract seems to hinge on a guess," said Oscar the Owl. if the queen of spades is a singleton, declarer can finesse against East's knave-to-three. If the trumps break two-two, declarer can bring them down by playing for the drop. Our friend is a good guesser, so ..."

"On the contrary," retorted H.H., "guessing is the worst part of my game. Nearly three per cent of the time I misguess. Fortunately, in this case, there was no need to guess at all. I allowed West to hold the queen of spades, knowing that he would lead another diamond. Had he not led a diamond, he would have doubtless returned a heart. All that matters is that he wouldn't have led a club, not after I told him that I had Papa's ace. And now you see," concluded the Hog, downing my Cognac, "that the contract simply depends on co-ordinating the bidding with the play."

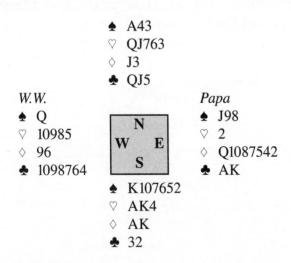

♠ A43
♥ QJ763
♦ J3
♣ QJ5

W.W.
♠ Q
♥ 10985
♦ 96
♣ 1098764

Papa
♠ J98
♥ 2
♦ Q1087542
♣ AK

♠ K107652
♥ AK4
♦ AK
♣ 32

"Honours even," pronounced the Owl. Papa fooled you by his clever defence this evening and you retaliated by imaginative bidding last Wednesday. Neither of you can be seriously blamed for being taken in by the other."

"You astound me," cried H.H., throwing someone's cigar into the fire, "don't you see that both West and East should have defeated me? Since Papa didn't double North's five diamond response to my Blackwood, he was surely steering his partner away from a diamond lead. West might have opened a heart, of course, but had he done so, he should have switched to a club when he came in with the queen of spades."

"That wasn't Papa's fault," pointed out O.O.

"True," agreed H.H., "but Papa erred badly by not playing the two of diamonds on the knave at trick one. He should have realised that the diamond position could have no bearing on the contract. If West had no entry, the slam was unbreakable, and if declarer had to give up a trick – a trump or a heart – a club return was imperative. Kindly note," went on the Hog, in case anyone had overlooked his brilliance, "that had I not covered the nine of diamonds with the knave, the Greek would have probably followed with the two, in which case West would have surely switched to a club. The Walrus may not know much about bridge, but he certainly knows about suit signals."

Chapter Eleven
The Hog Foots the Bill

"Anyone can play well these days," declared the Hideous Hog, putting down my glass. "It takes a master to know how to play badly."

With a gesture of distaste, the Hog signed the bill. It was his turn, or rather it had been for some time, and no one tried to stop him.

"Some contracts," went on H.H., despatching the last gaufrette, "can be made only against the best defence, just as some defences will succeed only if declarer is good enough to be bested.

"Kindly don't interrupt me" he snapped at the Rabbit, anticipating an interjection. "I know perfectly well the obvious point you are about to make, that my own inimi … er, my own defences, though admittedly the best, break unbreakable contracts, again and again. True," agreed the Hog, gracefully conceding the point, "but it's a question of knowing when to play well, and above all, when not to play too well. Now, here's an instructive hand for you. Give me something to write on. Anything will do."

Nervously, Timothy the Toucan clutched a morocco-bound volume of Nostrodamus's *Predictions*. He knew the Hog's habits. Only recently he had scrawled a three-card ending across a priceless misprint on the frontispiece of an ancient first edition.

"There," said the Hog, scribbling quickly. "You are West.

East/West Game. Dealer South.

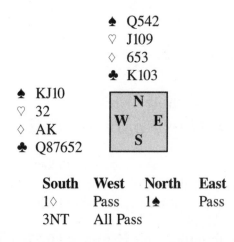

```
                    ♠ Q542
                    ♡ J109
                    ◇ 653
                    ♣ K103
   ♠ KJ10         ┌──────────┐
   ♡ 32           │    N     │
   ◇ AK           │  W    E  │
   ♣ Q87652       │    S     │
                  └──────────┘
```

South	West	North	East
1◇	Pass	1♠	Pass
3NT	All Pass		

"You lead a club. Declarer plays low from dummy and captures East's nine of clubs with his ace. Next comes the queen of diamonds and you are in. Proceed."

"Another club, of course," said the Toucan, bouncing in his chair, his long crimson nose aglow with the port.

"No" said the Rabbit firmly. "That's the sort of thing one does at the table. I mean, that's what I would do. It can't be right."

"Since the nine brought the ace, partner appears to have the knave," ventured Oscar the Owl cautiously.

"Exactly," agreed the Hog. "So what happens? Declarer naturally holds up, hoping that the diamond honours are split. Now, if East started with three clubs, communications between the defenders will have been cut. But since you have six clubs, you know that unless South's ace of clubs was bare, which is highly unlikely on the bidding, East started with the knave-nine of clubs precisely. His knave will win the trick, but he won't have another club to return, and what could be more frustrating than that."

"What did I tell you," chipped in the Rabbit. "No more clubs for me. I switch to a spade."

"No good," explained H.H. "South wouldn't have jumped to three no-trumps with nothing in spades. Besides, that would leave him with only sixteen points, not enough by any standard. So, you see, he simply must have the ace of spades. Come on. You have one entry left and there's no time to lose."

No one spoke. To relieve the tension, the Rabbit called for another bottle of port.

"There is a pretty solution," resumed the Hog after a while, "a play that is clever, yet simple and almost certain to succeed."

"Well, what do you do?" asked the Toucan eagerly.

"Try leading the queen of clubs," suggested the Hog. "You know that the knave of clubs is with partner, but declarer doesn't, so naturally, seeing the queen of clubs, he will place you with both honours and will duck in dummy. Simple, isn't it?"

"Brilliant. Terrific." The Rabbit and Toucan spoke at once.

"But in what way," asked the Owl, "does this fit in with what you were saying about contracts that can only be made against the best defence? Wasn't your queen of clubs the best?"

"Certainly," agreed the Hog, "but then, you see, surprisingly enough, declarer did make his contract.

This was the full deal:

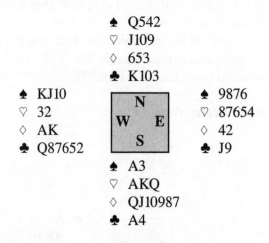

```
              ♠ Q542
              ♡ J109
              ◊ 653
              ♣ K103
♠ KJ10                      ♠ 9876
♡ 32          N            ♡ 87654
◊ AK      W       E        ◊ 42
♣ Q87652      S            ♣ J9
              ♠ A3
              ♡ AKQ
              ◊ QJ10987
              ♣ A4
```

"Declarer, who happened to be our friend the Walrus, went up with dummy's king of clubs, dropping East's knave, and proceeded to make eleven tricks."

"What made him go up ..." began O.O.

"I forgot to tell you," explained H.H., "who was sitting West. Papa, in person. No," he added, intercepting the Toucan's look of surprise. "I was East, the victim of Papa's infinite subtlety."

"This doesn't explain ..." the Owl began again.

"Oh, but it does," interrupted the Hog, "because Papa was, as usual, too clever. I told you that the lead was a club. What I didn't tell you was that Themistocles had cunningly selected the two of clubs! Yes, as I've said before, that Greek would false card with a singleton. But observe the effect. Duly deceived by the lead, the Walrus expected the clubs to break four-four. This he could well afford, but if he allowed the queen of clubs to hold, a spade switch could be dangerous, so why should he run a needless risk? Papa wasn't satisfied with one piece of deception, he brought off two, so successfully that they cancelled each other out."

The Dangers of Playing Too Well

"I'll show you another hand," went on the Hog, passing the port round to himself, "but do give me a bit of paper, someone." No room remained on the back of the bill and, screwing it up in a ball, the Hog consigned it to the ashtray.

"Thank you," said H.H., grabbing the Rabbit's pocket diary. "Don't worry," he added, brushing aside R.R.'s pleas to be careful. "I'll find a space. You are East this time. There:

East/West Game. Dealer West.

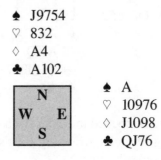

    ♠ J9754
    ♡ 832
    ♢ A4
    ♣ A102

    ♠ A
    ♡ 10976
    ♢ J1098
    ♣ QJ76

West	North	East	South
Pass	Pass	Pass	1♠
Pass	3♠	Pass	4♠
All Pass			

"West leads the king of hearts, the ace and then the five of hearts. Declarer follows with the four and the knave and wins the third trick with the queen of hearts. Crossing to the ace of diamonds, he leads the knave of spades and you are in. What do you play?"

"A diamond stands out a mile. So you probably want me to lead a club," said R.R. "I wonder why?"

With a contemptuous grunt, H.H. turned to T.T. "Surely a diamond can't hurt," pleaded the Toucan.

Oscar the Owl blinked noncommittally.

"What do you think of the trump position?" persisted the Hog.

"Declarer appears to be missing an honour," replied O.O. thoughtfully. "He may be looking for the queen of spades or he may be hoping to crash the ace and king of spades. With an indifferent player sitting East ..."

"East was not indifferent," broke in the Hog. "He was a fine player and could see that if West had the king of spades or the Qxx, for that matter, the contract would go down anyway. But if he had a doubleton queen, there wasn't a moment to lose, for as soon as declarer gained the lead, he would bring down that queen. So East returned the thirteenth heart to allow West to make his queen of spades *en passant*, if ..."

"I knew all along that you'd find a way! With you as East, declarer hadn't a hope," cried the Toucan excitedly.

"Papa was East. I was South," corrected the Hog, tearing out another sheet from the diary to write in the other hands.

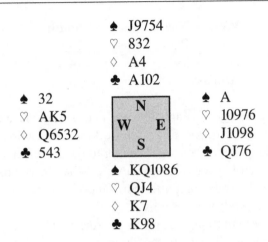

"I played as I did," explained H.H., "hoping that if Papa had ace and another spade, he would duck, in case West had a singleton honour, just as you suggested Oscar. Then I would have cashed my king of diamonds, and with the red suits eliminated, I would have thrown Papa in with the ace of spades, forcing him to open up the clubs. I thought that was my only chance, and so it would have been against a less far-sighted defender. But you see how dangerous it can be to play too well. Against a less-gifted defender I would have had no chance."

Success for the Mediocre

The waiter came up with a newly made out bill, putting it down, through force of habit, before the Rueful Rabbit.

The Hog was busy setting out another hand. "You are back in West's seat," he told us, "and since you are always putting me in the wrong place, let me tell you from the start that I was South."

Game All. Dealer West.

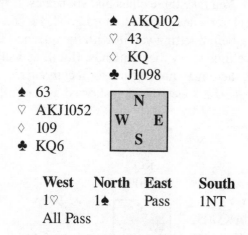

- ♠ AKQ102
- ♡ 43
- ◇ KQ
- ♣ J1098

- ♠ 63
- ♡ AKJ1052
- ◇ 109
- ♣ KQ6

West	North	East	South
1♡	1♠	Pass	1NT
All Pass			

"You lead the king of hearts to which partner follows with the six and your humble servant with the eight. What do you do next?"

"A diamond," suggested the Toucan in a tremulous voice.

R.R. shook his head. A nostril quivered suspiciously. No one asked questions unless there was a catch somewhere. Probably the answer was to underlead the ace of hearts, though for the life of him he couldn't think why.

"Let me help you," offered the Hog. "If declarer wins the next trick, he may be able to reel off six more before letting you in. So, while you have the chance, you must try to get partner in for a heart lead through the closed hand."

All nodded in agreement. Even O.O. forgot to look inscrutable.

"If declarer has both the missing aces," continued the Hog, "there's precious little hope anyway. But there's a good chance on the bidding that East has one of them. Which one shall it be?"

"It could be either, but it's safer to try a diamond than a club," ventured the Toucan.

"Neither is safe," retorted H.H., "which is why you should try both."

"Of course," agreed T.T. enthusiastically.

"How?" asked R.R.

"Lead the king of clubs," replied H.H. "If partner has the ace of clubs, all is well. You take three clubs and six hearts. If the king of clubs falls to declarer's ace it does him no good. He can only take five more tricks, before letting you in with the queen of clubs, and there will still be time to try the diamonds. But if, at trick two, you lead a diamond, there may not be time for a club later."

Tearing out another sheet, the Hog showed us the full deal.

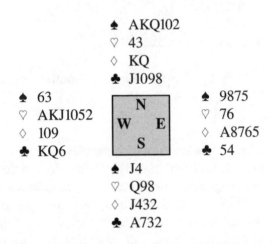

♠ AKQ102
♥ 43
♦ KQ
♣ J1098

♠ 63
♥ AKJ1052
♦ 109
♣ KQ6

♠ 9875
♥ 76
♦ A8765
♣ 54

♠ J4
♥ Q98
♦ J432
♣ A732

"And did West lead the king of clubs?" asked Oscar.

"Certainly," replied the Hog. "West was Papa. He may not be the second best player in the world, as he likes to think, but he is far too good to lead a diamond blindly."

"So the contract was defeated?" asked the Toucan.

"Aren't you forgetting," rejoined the Hog sternly, "that I was declarer? Do you expect me to go down? Of course not. I had two excellent cards, those little baby clubs, and I put them to good use. On Papa's king of clubs, I played the seven. With the three and two of clubs missing from the trick, the four of clubs looked like a come-on signal. Papa led another club and that was that. Observe that even I couldn't have made that contract against a thoughtless defence.

"What a wonderful host you are, R.R.," said the Hog with a courtly bow, returning the Rabbit's diary. "It's always a pleasure to dine with you."

"Oh, I say," cried the Rabbit, shocked to find that the Hog had been tearing out pages with addresses and telephone numbers. "Look what you've done!"

"Mathilda de Montmorency," read out the Hog, unscrewing a bit of paper. "How ridiculous! I bet that's not her real name. A psyche, I expect. Ha! Ha!"

Chapter Twelve
Every Picture Tells a Story

"This is an outrage," cried the Hideous Hog. Never had I seen him in such a fury. He had just opened his mail in the bar of the Unicorn and staring at him from inside the folds of brown paper, midway between the almonds and the olives, was a signed photo of Papa, twelve inches by four. Pinned to it was a photocopy of a letter signed by Jupiter Jones, Honorary Secretary of the Caccippuma Fund.

"I will report that unspeakable Greek to the police. I will sue him. I will have questions asked in the House," thundered H.H., passing, or rather hurling at me, the letter.

Barely had ten days elapsed since the Gala Individual held at the Unicorn to raise funds for Caccippuma – the Cash and Credits Cooperative for the Initiation of Primitive Peoples into the Use of Modern Arms. Donor of the first prize was a distinguished transatlantic member, head of Outer Space Development Inc. of New York. He had presented a 10,000-acre estate on the moon, 'quiet, secluded, unspoilt by man, superbly situated between the Sea of Tribulation and the Lake of Calamity', in the words of the brochure.

The Rueful Rabbit, who had started the Individual at 100-1, with no takers, donated to the lofty cause a case of vintage Krug for the player with the best slam record. The Hideous Hog, an easy winner, contributed, in turn, an autographed picture of himself as a prize for the competitor who scored the greatest number of cold bottoms.

"There is no particle of skill in this Individual nonsense. It is sheer unadulterated luck," protested the embittered Greek when the Hog's picture was formally presented to him. "Every player in the room set out to fix me and all won hands down."

"Oh! Come, come," jeered the Hog. "The champagne I happened to win is an ephemeral trifle. Once drunk 'tis soon forgotten. But the picture of a master is a source of inspiration which lives forever. Indeed, Papa, you are to be envied."

That is how it all started.

I took up the letter which had come with Papa's photo and read:

Dear Mr Themistocles Papadopoulos,

My Committee wishes me to thank you and your distinguished friend, who so modestly desires to be known only by the initials H.H., for donating to our great cause the magnificent trophies you both won at the Unicorn Bridge Individual.

We have not yet come to a decision in regard to the striking futuristic picture which was your own prize, but your illustrious friend will be glad to know that the case of champagne, which we owe to his generosity, is to be awarded to the Neatest Needle in the National Knitting Contest open to all members of the ex-Gentlewomen's Association.

"Monstrous impudence," fumed H.H., "throwing away the champagne I earned by the sweat of my brow. But fear not. No ex-gentlewoman is going to get tipsy on my Krug. I'll write to Jupiter. I'll cable. I'll go to him myself," rampaged the indignant Hog.

I looked again at Papa's picture. Without a doubt his lips were curving upwards in a triumphant smile. Thinking back on the Individual, I could not suppress a tinge of sympathy for the Hog, who had tried so valiantly to win the champagne. Maybe the cards were not shuffled as thoroughly as they should have been that night. Maybe it was just coincidence. Whatever the reason, unusually big hands were out and the intrepid Hog shot his way into one slam after another.

Stretching a Point

On the first of these Walter the Walrus was his partner. Strange faces – two of the many which appeared from nowhere to grace the Gala – sat on either side of him. Walter opened two no-trumps and raised the Hog's three spades to four. Thinking no doubt of the Krug, the Hideous Hog bid a confident six spades. These were the four hands:

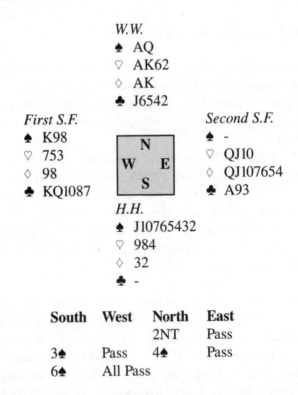

W.W.
♠ AQ
♡ AK62
◇ AK
♣ J6542

First S.F.
♠ K98
♡ 753
◇ 98
♣ KQ1087

Second S.F.
♠ -
♡ QJ10
◇ QJ107654
♣ A93

H.H.
♠ J10765432
♡ 984
◇ 32
♣ -

South	West	North	East
		2NT	Pass
3♠	Pass	4♠	Pass
6♠	All Pass		

"You owe me a trump, Walter," said the Hog severely when dummy went down. It was good tactics for, if the slam failed, the Walrus would certainly bring up the question of points and the Hog's count was comparatively low.

The first Strange Face, sitting West, led the king of clubs and it looked to the kibitzers as if the slam would depend on one of two things: catching the king of trumps or a four-four club break which would allow declarer to dispose of his losing heart. That was what I heard Oscar the Owl whisper to Peregrine the Penguin.

The Hog ruffed the opening club and finessed the spade. Dummy's queen held, but East, the second Strange Face, showed out.

"So much for catching the king of trumps," murmured Oscar.

H.H. ruffed a second club, crossed to dummy with a diamond and ruffed a club again. Returning to dummy with his second diamond, the Hog trumped a fourth club. As East threw a diamond, Oscar and Peregrine sagely shook their heads, as if to say: "Unlucky hand. Nothing works."

The Hog now entered dummy with the ace of hearts and ruffed the last club. Then came the king of hearts followed by dummy's two. With three cards left this was the position:

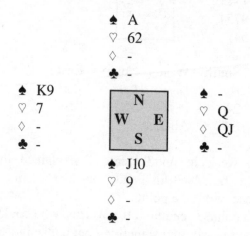

East led a diamond, perforce, and H.H. ruffed with the ten, leaving West with the choice of underruffing or having his king smothered by the ace. Either way the Hideous Hog was home.

The Walrus, heaving heavily from side to side, was about to say something. The Hog forestalled him: "I didn't quite have the regulation point count," he admitted handsomely, "but with a ten-card suit, you know, one must stretch things a little."

Entries Galore

A few hands later Molly the Mule was on the Hog's right. Papa was his left-hand opponent and the Rueful Rabbit was his partner. I was sitting between Papa and the Rabbit when this board came up.

East/West Game. Dealer South.

R.R.
♠ 654
♡ 876
◇ KJ32
♣ K87

Papa
♠ KQJ
♡ J543
◇ 9754
♣ 54

```
      N
   W     E
      S
```

South	West	North	East
H.H.	*Papa*	*R.R.*	*M.M.*
2♣	Pass	2NT	Pass
6♣	All Pass		

"I am a little weak in middle cards," explained the Rabbit apologetically, as he tabled his hand, "but I didn't like to give a negative response with nine points."

"Which nine points?" enquired the Walrus, who could only see seven. The Rabbit nearly said something but blinked instead.

"Thank you, partner," said the Hog pleasantly. Papa, who had placed the king of spades on the table, looked up suspiciously, sensing something underhand behind the Hog's uncalled-for civility.

The Hog won the trick with the ace and slowly peeled off seven clubs. Molly, who had played the ten of spades at trick one, threw the nine, eight and seven, to give Papa the count.

I tried to follow Papa's thoughts. Which five cards should he keep to the end? The Hog was marked with ten black cards, two red aces and one other card, presumably a diamond. The Greek began by discarding two hearts, the five then the three, to let the Mule count the suit.

The Hog couldn't have the queen of diamonds, as well as the ace, for he would then have thirteen top tricks, and if Molly had queen to three diamonds, the contract was doomed – so long as there was no confusion in the discards.

Having shed her spades, Molly the Mule threw the ten of hearts, then the six of diamonds. Papa frowned. Had his delicate signal in hearts escaped her? Was she trying to deceive declarer? Whatever the reason, she was clearly keeping a heart too many and a diamond too few. Coming down to six cards, when the last of the Hog's seven clubs appeared on the table, Papa remained with queen-knave of spades, knave-four of hearts and nine-seven of diamonds.

He had intended throwing a diamond, but after Molly's thoughtless discard that would be suicidal. The Hog would cash the ace and seeing him show out on the next round he would willy-nilly bring down the queen, scoring the knave of diamonds as his twelfth trick. So the Greek let go the four of hearts. The Hog could still make the right guess, of course, but Papa would do what he could to protect partner's queen.

Molly's look on seeing the four of hearts would have done credit to Medusa. Unable to contain my curiosity any longer, I went round the table to see what was happening. This was the complete deal:

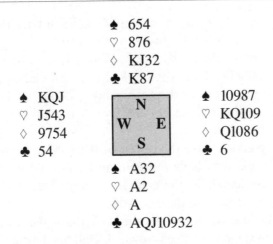

♠ 654
♡ 876
◊ KJ32
♣ K87

♠ KQJ
♡ J543
◊ 9754
♣ 54

♠ 10987
♡ KQ109
◊ Q1086
♣ 6

♠ A32
♡ A2
◊ A
♣ AQJ10932

After following to the ace of spades and to seven clubs, the Mule was left with the king-queen of hearts and queen-ten-eight of diamonds. The nine of hearts had been her last, fateful discard. The Hog promptly cashed the two red aces and exited with a heart, forcing a diamond from Molly into dummy's king-knave on which H.H. gratefully parked his two losing spades.

"Why did you unguard your queen of diamonds?" cried Papa.

"I did no such thing," retorted Molly, angrily. "Why did *you* endplay me? Had you kept a second heart, instead of that fatuous diamond, I could have thrown my top hearts, allowing you to win the trick with your knave and ..."

With a friendly leer at the kibitzers, the Hog, wreathed in smiles, addressed the Rabbit. "You showed excellent judgment, R.R., in taking two extra points for your knave of diamonds. It was worth all three of them."

It had occurred to neither defender that the Hog would cut himself off from dummy, leaving the king-knave of diamonds to which he had no longer access, to mesmerise and bewitch.

"I have yet to meet a man who'll admit that he's in the wrong," snorted the Mule, as she rose to leave the table.

Papa gulped. "So long as they have the last word, that's all they care about," added Molly, and with a scathing look at the Greek she walked, or rather marched, away.

Chapter Thirteen
Election Time

"I suppose he's all right," said Peregrine the Penguin uneasily.

We were all puzzled by the Hog's unusual behaviour. First he was heard being civil to the Walrus. Then, apropos of nothing at all, he had been polite to the Toucan. And finally, just before reminding us to order him drinks as he went to the telephone, he said of Papa: "A good player, that Greek. It's a pleasure to take his money," and he said it as if he meant it.

"All very much out of character, isn't it?" chipped in Colin the Corgi, joining the conversation. "And yet the reason isn't hard to find. Remember that H.H. has put forward his candidature for election to the committee."

On the face of it, that, too, was out of character. The Hog had no, time for what he described as 'platonic activities', and sitting on committees was one of them. But he had to protect his interests and there was an ominous move afoot to limit side-bets on the rubber, which, often out of proportion to the stakes, were apt to distort the play. As a member of the committee H.H. could use his position to promote what he regarded as the beneficent processes of a free economy.

"At election time," observed the Corgi, "politeness to partners, like kissing babies, is an acceptable form of prostitution."

"Praising Papa is overdoing it, surely," objected O.O.

"H.H. has had good reason recently," rejoined C.C. with a chuckle, "to be impressed by Papa's skill." As he spoke he wrote down a hand. "Opponents, that's Papa and Karapet, had just collected a hefty penalty. Unfortunately for the Hog, his partner, the Walrus, had picked up a twenty-point hand, which meant that he couldn't stop bidding till he was doubled. So the side was badly down already when Karapet opened two clubs."

Game All. Dealer East.

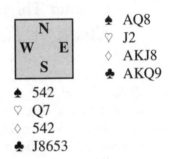

♠ AQ8
♡ J2
◇ AKJ8
♣ AKQ9

♠ 542
♡ Q7
◇ 542
♣ J8653

South	West	North	East
H.H.	*Papa*	*W.W.*	*Karapet*
			2♣
Pass	2♠	Pass	3♠
Pass	4NT	Pass	5♠
Pass	6♡	Pass	7♠
All Pass			

Oscar the Owl viewed dummy with disapproval. "I don't like that three spades bid," he said. "Karapet should have called two no-trumps, pinpointing his shape and strength."

Peregrine the Penguin nodded gravely in acquiescence. "Was six hearts a substitute for Josephine?" he asked.

"Yes," replied the Corgi. "Blackwood having been invoked, five notrumps would be an enquiry for kings. To call for the grand slam if Karapet had two of the three top honours, Papa had to do something else. I agree with you about Karapet's rebid, but the point of the hand is in the play. The lead was the ten of hearts to the knave, queen and king. Papa proceeded to cash the ace of hearts and at trick three ruffed a heart with one of dummy's honours. What are the chances, would you say, of breaking the contract?"

The Corgi sat back. The Owl nodded sagely. The Penguin concurred.

"Clearly," prompted C.C., "if declarer has either five spades or the queen of diamonds, he has thirteen top tricks, so we must assume that he has neither."

"The diamond finesse being right," interjected O.O., "he can't go wrong. After testing the clubs and finding that they didn't break, he is bound to go for the diamonds."

"True," agreed the Corgi, "but what if declarer has reason to believe that the queen of diamonds is wrong, that the Hog has that card?"

"Why should he believe any such thing?" objected the Penguin.

"Because the shadow can be more convincing that the substance," replied C.C. "And this was where H.H. was lucky to have Papa as his opponent. No one but an expert could fail to make the contract, but against a master of Papa's calibre there was a way and the Hog found it."

"On that rubbish?" broke in P.P. incredulously.

"Well, no, not on *quite* that rubbish," rejoined the Corgi. "Mentally he transposed a little club into a little spade and the five of diamonds into the queen. His hand, his fantasy hand, was now:

♠ 5 4 3 2 ♡ Q 7 ◇ Q 4 2 ♣ J 8 6 5."

The Owl blinked noncommittally, wondering what the Corgi was leading up to.

"What would H.H. discard at trick three on that heart ruffed in dummy," went on C.C., "if he had that holding? In effect, he would be squeezed in the minors – unless he threw a trump! Then, discarding after dummy on declarer's trumps, he would be in no trouble."

"And did he really throw a trump?" enquired the Owl.

"He did," replied C.C., "and now put yourself in Papa's place. Accepting the image projected by the Hog," pursued Colin, "Papa reasoned that if he had to throw a trump it could only be because he had the queen of diamonds and four clubs, and if so, the contract could be made by means of a Vienna Coup."

This was the deal as Papa saw it, as the Hog wanted him to see it.

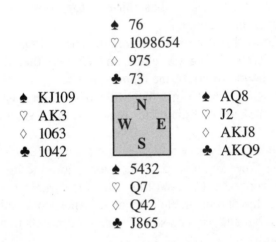

```
                    ♠ 76
                    ♡ 1098654
                    ◊ 975
                    ♣ 73
  ♠ KJ109                        ♠ AQ8
  ♡ AK3          N               ♡ J2
  ◊ 1063       W   E             ◊ AKJ8
  ♣ 1042          S              ♣ AKQ9
                    ♠ 5432
                    ♡ Q7
                    ◊ Q42
                    ♣ J865
```

"So at trick four," pursued Colin the Corgi, "Papa cashed the ace of spades, laid down the ace-king of diamonds, and proceeded to take three rounds of trumps, leaving himself with the ten of diamonds and the ten-four-two of clubs, and dummy with the ace-king-queen-nine of clubs. Now the fantasy hand, unable to retain the queen of diamonds and four clubs in the four-card ending, was well and truly squeezed. When the queen of diamonds didn't show up, Papa turned confidently to the clubs and … curtains.

"To this day," concluded the Corgi, "the Walrus doesn't know what happened. 'Some of these virtuosos can't take a simple, finesse and yet they take my money. Tcha,' he growled in disgust. Poor Karapet took it stoically. 'Even when a finesse is right it still fails,' was his only comment. Who would be a Djoulikyan?"

"A very imaginative defence," agreed O.O., "but H.H. was lucky to find Papa with the ten of diamonds, setting the stage for a Vienna Coup."

"Not as lucky as all that," replied C.C. "The squeeze would still function if H.H. had four diamonds, whoever had the ten, for the Walrus would then have a doubleton. The luck was to be up against a declarer good enough to go down."

The Two-Card Trick

As he spoke Colin was writing down another hand. "A very different situation here," he explained, "but once again the Hog had reason to be grateful for Papa's expertise. Allowing for side-bets, it was worth, I should say, at least four bottles of vintage Bollinger. There you are:

Game All. Dealer West.

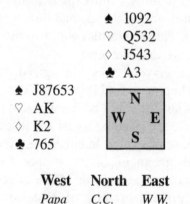

```
                ♠ 1092
                ♡ Q532
                ◊ J543
                ♣ A3
  ♠ J87653      ┌─────────┐
  ♡ AK          │    N    │
  ◊ K2          │  W   E  │
  ♣ 765         │    S    │
                └─────────┘
```

West	North	East	South
Papa	*C.C.*	*W W.*	*H.H.*
1♠	Pass	Pass	3♡
Pass	4♡	All Pass	

"I was playing with the Hog, you will observe, and ended up as dummy. Papa started with the ace of hearts, then the king of hearts. The first time the Walrus followed, but to the second trick he threw the queen of clubs. Papa continued with the six of spades, the Walrus produced the queen and the Hog won with the king. Now came a club to dummy's ace and another to the king in the closed hand, Walter following with the four, then the knave. Next came the ace of diamonds."

The Corgi paused. "I hope," he said, "that I am not going too fast for you. We've had two rounds of trumps, one spade, the ace of clubs, the king of clubs and now, at trick six, the ace of diamonds and it's Papa to play."

It was a little while before anyone spoke. Then, straightening his dark orange tie, the Penguin called for attention.

"The play," he began, "conforms closely to the classical elimination pattern. Let us see if we can build up a picture of declarer's cards. We know that he started with six hearts since Walter showed out on the second round. We have seen two clubs. If he had another he would have doubtless ruffed it in dummy, so presumably he had a doubleton.

"Similarly, if he had two spades only, he could have cashed the ace of spades and ruffed dummy's third spade in his own hand. Since he hasn't, we must conclude that he had three spades, to be precise the ace-king-four. This leaves him with two diamonds, the ace, which is now before us, and one other."

Oscar the Owl nodded gravely. "Yes," he agreed. "The Hog's plan is pretty clear. He is hoping to find Papa with a doubleton king or queen of diamonds. If so, Papa will be thrown in at trick seven and compelled to lead a club, conceding a ruff and discard, or else to play away from his knave of spades. In either event the Hog will get an extra trick." Raising an imperious flipper, the Penguin signalled that he was about to speak again. "Papa can counter the endplay," he said, "by throwing his king of diamonds under the ace. The next diamond will be won by East, who will lead another, forcing the Hog to ruff and to lead spades himself."

"It's all very well thinking out these clever things afterwards," protested the Rabbit, "but how can you tell what everyone is up to *at the time*? I mean, one doesn't always know what one is up to oneself and when you have to play quickly and everything, well …"

"Then you'll be glad to know," the Corgi told him, "that Papa didn't hesitate a split second. No sooner had the Hog released from his hand the ace of diamonds than Papa sent the king of diamonds racing after it. They landed on the table together."

"Brilliant," gasped the Rabbit in admiration. "Fancy working everything out and finding the solution on the spur of the moment. No wonder H.H. had a word of praise for him."

O.O. and P.P. raised sceptical eyebrows. The Hog liked to put first things first and that left him little time to praise other people.

"When you have before you the full deal," said Colin the Corgi, "you will see, I think, why H.H. was so magnanimous." These were the four hands:

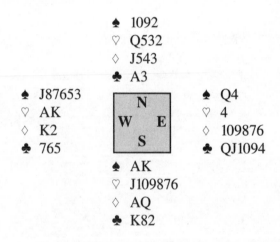

♠ 1092
♡ Q532
◊ J543
♣ A3

♠ J87653
♡ AK
◊ K2
♣ 765

♠ Q4
♡ 4
◊ 109876
♣ QJ1094

♠ AK
♡ J109876
◊ AQ
♣ K82

"Rather neat, don't you think?" went on the Corgi. "The Hog, who keeps a running total, hand by hand, just as I do, could see that the rubber would be a wash-out if he made no more than ten tricks. For money to change hands, so that he could win his considerable side-bets, he needed an extra trick and he could be certain from the bidding, having seen Walter's queen of spades, that Papa had the king of diamonds. So what does he do? He stages a pseudo-elimination, arranges for Papa to miscount his hand and persuades him to throw away his king of diamonds. Of course, only a good player would fall for it."

"The two-card trick. Very ingenious," said P.P., "and yet it wasn't altogether unlucky to find a doubleton king of diamonds."

Colin shook his head. "Not really," he replied, "Papa was marked with long spades since he had none of the tops. He had shown two hearts and he followed upwards in clubs. More likely than not, he had a doubleton diamond. The contract, of course, was never in doubt, but it was a pretty way to win a wager and shows, incidentally," concluded the Corgi, "how large side-bets can affect the play. I doubt if H.H. would have wasted so cunning a stratagem for one point on the rubber. He would have kept it up his sleeve for another day."

Chapter 14
How are your Reflexes?

Meditatively stroking his chin, Oscar the Owl repeated to himself *sotto voce*: "West leads the five of clubs and South to lose against any defence."

"What's it all about?" asked the Toucan, breaking in on the Owl's soliloquy.

"It's a new type of problem", explained O.O., pointing to a diagram in the evening paper. "I have to work out the contract and to plan declarer's misplay."

♠ A43
♡ 87
◊ QJ109
♣ A982

♠ 765
♡ AKQJ109
◊ A2
♣ Q10

T.T. looked at the hand critically. There seemed to be no good reason why anyone should go down in anything. "Could it be four spades or something odd, after a psychic opening, perhaps?"

"No, no," replied Oscar, "everything must be reasonable. No psychics, no lunatics."

"Oh, so it's not the Rabbit," said T.T. with relief, but the solution still eluded him.

As we pondered, the Hideous Hog and Walter the Walrus joined us in the bar.

"Curious," said W.W., poring over the problem. "All in all, the North/South hands add up to a fullblooded 30 points – not enough for a slam but far too much not to make game. So how does one lose it? There must be a coup. Perhaps declarer should smother dummy or endplay himself or ..."

The Hog looked at him with the scorn he usually reserved for partners.

"Allow me to help you, Walter," he said with a gentle sneer. "We might be hard put to it to lose five tricks in no-trumps. So let's try four hearts. We are told that West opens the five of clubs. We'll call the cards in turn, you and I, trick by trick. You go first."

"The two," called the Walrus.

H.H. bowed low to the Owl. "You have your solution," he announced. "Walter has smothered his dummy, broken his contract and solved the problem for you – though unintentionally, I fear, so he cannot really claim the credit for it."

"It will be interesting to see the full deal in tomorrow's paper," observed Timothy the Toucan.

"Why?" asked the Hog. "The problem is to lose the contract and Walter's way is surely the best. Just give East the king of clubs, and the rest of the distribution doesn't matter. He wins the first trick – the king of clubs could even be a singleton – and returns a spade, driving out dummy's ace before the diamonds are set up. As happens so often, declarer, butchers his contract at trick one. The defence isn't called upon to do anything."

"I didn't have to play that two," protested the Walrus. "I spoke too quickly. I ... er ... didn't mean ..."

"On the contrary," retorted the Hog. "You did mean and you had to play the two of clubs. That's just it, don't you see. It looked right. It felt right, and most of the time it would have been right, too. Playing low from dummy was an automatic reflex, an inner compulsion to do the right thing even though it was wrong."

"But surely ..." began T.T.

"Yes, surely ..." echoed W.W.

"Not at all," declared H.H., rejecting the arguments which were about to be put forward. "Why do you make the game so difficult? Most of the mistakes at bridge are obvious ones – as soon as you spot them, that is. Oscar's problem is no exception, but it points a moral. People who make the right play automatically, without malice aforethought, often live to regret it. Conversely, a well-planned absurdity may succeed because no one allows for it. Now here are a couple of hands to illustrate both sides of the medal:

```
            ♠ Q75
            ♡ J10
            ◇ QJ109876
            ♣ 10
```

```
            N
        W       E
            S
```

```
            ♠ A10
            ♡ AQ2
            ◇ AK
            ♣ AJ9872
```

South	West	North	East
		3◇	Pass
3NT	All Pass		

"It's your turn, Timothy, to call the cards. You are South. West opens the six of spades against your three no-trumps. You play dummy's seven of spades and South covers with the eight of spades. Go on from there."

The Toucan bounced up and down in his armchair. The rhythmic movement helped him to think. "Trick one – ten of spades. Tricks two and three – ace and king of diamonds. Trick four – queen of hearts." T.T. looked up expectantly.

"Go on," said the Hog, "all follow and you've made four tricks. Only five more to go."

"I, er … no, I don't. I …"

"It doesn't matter what you don't do," interrupted H.H. brutally. "You did your best to kill the hand at trick one, just as Walter did on the previous deal and for exactly the same reason. An inner voice told you not to waste the ace of spades on the eight when the ten would do. Now you can't get at dummy's diamonds and you'll need a lot of luck in the black suits to get home, but there are no miracles, not even small ones, so down you go."

The Walrus opened his mouth. He was probably about to say something, but the Hog stopped him in time. "No, Walter," he told him firmly, "we are no longer trying to lose the contract, so your contribution is unlikely to be helpful."

"What should I have done?" asked T.T. meekly.

"You should have won the first trick with the ace of spades, not with the ten," said H.H. "Then, after cashing the ace and king of diamonds you should have played back that ten, hoping to find West with the king. A heart or a spade from him would let you into dummy, as might a small club, and a high club would allow you to make five club tricks. The whole thing is just like taking a simple finesse. You play for a particular card to be well placed. That's all."

"A fifty-fifty chance," boomed the Walrus, who fancied himself as a mathematician.

"If the six of spades is a true lead it's nearer a hundred per cent," replied the Hog, "and even if it isn't, it's still the best chance."

"And did you in fact, win the eight with the ace?" asked the Toucan admiringly.

"Certainly," replied the Hog. "Who do you take me for? I mean, that's what I should have done had I been South. As it happens, I was North."

Papa's Good Luck

We registered the surprise expected of us and H.H. explained.

"I was playing with Papa. He's enjoying a good run just at present and cuts me at least half the time. Mind you, I don't object. One has to work out one's bad luck somehow and if I didn't cut Papa I'd break a leg or something. It would come to the same thing in the end. Anyway, I opened three diamonds, Papa bid three no-trumps and when East doubled, I retreated into four diamonds. After all, why should he play every hand? But just because he'd been dummy twice or three times already that rubber, Themistocles lost his temper. At the top of his voice he bellowed seven diamonds, and before North and South had finished doubling, he redoubled. If he couldn't play the hand, he was going to make me pay for it. I had half a mind to convert to seven no-trumps just to see him squirm, but one mustn't be uncharitable, not at £2 a 100."

"Hardly a good contract," observed the Toucan, looking at the four hands.

"Nine points short," noted the Walrus, disapprovingly. "What did it cost?"

(hand rotated for convenience)

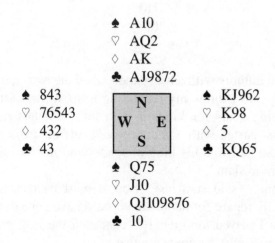

South	West	North	East
3◇	Pass	3NT	Dble
4◇	Pass	7◇	Dble
Pass	Pass	Rdble	All Pass

"The four of clubs was led," said the Hog ignoring the question. "I won with the ace and ruffed a club. Returning to dummy with the ace of trumps, I ruffed a second club. Then I repeated the process – a trump to the king and another club ruff, setting up two long clubs in dummy. There was still a trump out, so I drew it, throwing the ten of spades from the table and leaving this position:

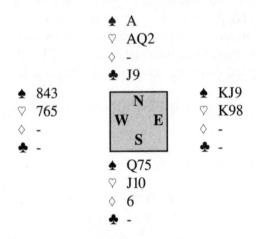

"I crossed to dummy with a heart and cashed the two clubs. On the penultimate club I threw my remaining heart while East let go a spade, keeping doubleton kings in both suits. The last club was a killer. If East parted with a heart I would ruff the two and set up the queen. So he bared his king of spades and my queen brought home the grand slam."

"Poor Papa," said someone, "how it must have hurt him. If you'd had any regard for his feelings you'd have gone down."

"Perhaps I played too quickly," conceded the Hog graciously. Already he was writing down another hand.

Wrong views

♠ 1043
♥ 9853
♦ 8763
♣ J4

```
      N
  W       E
      S
```

♠ A95
♥ K42
♦ Q5
♣ AKQ62

West	North	East	South
1♦	Pass	1♠	1NT

"West opens the king of diamonds, doesn't like his partner's two and switches to the two of spades on which East plays the king. How do you propose to make seven tricks?"

"There's no future in ducking," observed Oscar philosophically. "A diamond would come back bringing down the queen and, well, it wouldn't be so good."

"If we cash all our clubs," broke in the Toucan hopefully, "something may happen. It often does, you know, when people cash things against me."

W.W. wasn't impressed. "I cross to dummy with my knave of clubs and lead a heart. If East has the ace, I'm home. It's rather like the last hand the first time round ..."

"Almost identical," agreed the Hideous Hog, "the only point of difference is that on that occasion we had every reason to expect the king to be on the right side of the ace, where, as this time we know – *we know*," repeated the Hog accentuating the words, "that it's on the wrong side."

The Walrus wheezed. The Toucan gulped.

"What! You can't see it?" exclaimed the Hog. "Then shut your eyes, look at West's hand and think of the bidding. What did he intend to rebid over partner's response of one spade? He wasn't strong enough to reverse into two hearts or he wouldn't have passed. A raise in spades? Hardly. East has shown four or more and looking across the table we can see six our way. Clubs can be ruled out, too. It's our suit. No, clearly he intended to rebid one no-trump and to do that, playing a weak no trump, he would need fifteen to sixteen points. Well, count them. In spades, two – no more, for he would have led the queen, not the two, from QJ2. Eight points are hidden from view in diamonds. Give West the lot, bringing his total to ten. Now you see why he must have the ace of hearts. Without it, he would be short of the barest minimum for his one no-trump rebid."

"You needn't look at me as if it's my fault," cried the Walrus. "If West has the ace of hearts it's no use playing East for it. I agree. But what do you expect me to do about it?"

"To play West for it, of course," snapped back the Hog contemptuously.

"How?" cried T.T. and W.W. Two minor kibitzers gurgled sympathetically.

"At Trick 3," replied H.H., "you play the king of hearts-from your hand, just like that, expecting it to hold."

"Why should it?" asked T.T. incredulously.

"Absurd," agreed W.W.

"Certainly," admitted H.H. "So much so, in fact, that no one will suspect you of doing it. And now put yourself in West's place. He is a reasonable man and expects you to be reasonable, too, and to lead out an unsupported king isn't reasonable. So he will assume instinctively that you have the queen of hearts as well."

"But why shouldn't he take it just the same?" objected Oscar. "His ace will only make once."

The Hog shook his head. "West doesn't know that your queen of diamonds will drop or that his partner has the knave of spades or how the clubs are divided. So what should he lead if he goes up with the ace of hearts? No prospect pleases. He would much rather that you played away from something, if only your imaginary queen of hearts. Can you really blame him for ducking? Look at his hand."

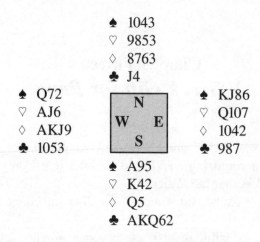

```
              ♠ 1043
              ♡ 9853
              ◊ 8763
              ♣ J4
  ♠ Q72                    ♠ KJ86
  ♡ AJ6      N             ♡ Q107
  ◊ AKJ9   W   E           ◊ 1042
  ♣ 1053     S             ♣ 987
              ♠ A95
              ♡ K42
              ◊ Q5
              ♣ AKQ62
```

"I should never have thought of playing it that way," admitted the Toucan, "but of course it's easy enough for West to take a wrong view."

"Everyone does that at times," agreed the Walrus.

"Almost everyone," corrected the Hog.

Chapter Fifteen
A Greek Gift for Papa

"Oh, well played H.H.!" said Oscar the Owl, our Senior Kibitzer.

"Just like a conjuring trick! And to think that I only had four points," cried Walter the Walrus.

"Amazing!" exclaimed Timothy the Toucan, bouncing in his chair.

There was a familiar hiss as the long sinewy legs of the Emeritus Professor of Bio-Sophistry, known to us all as the Secretary Bird on account of his appearance, emerged stealthily from behind a pillar.

"So," he observed with an engaging sneer, "H.H. is once more the centre of admiration. What miracle, I wonder, has he performed this time."

The table had broken up. Papa the Greek had just left and the rest of us, players and kibitzers, were mulling over the last hand as we toyed with a bottle of Madeira. While the Secretary Bird went on chatting in witty vein, the Hideous Hog ripped the latest announcement off the notice board and drew on the back the familiar diagram. With a malevolent gleam in his beady eyes, he set out in large, bold symbols the four hands. Then he obliged me by taking a cigarette and, putting the sheet down in the middle of the table, looked around for a match.

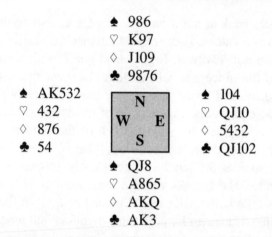

♠ 986
♡ K97
◇ J109
♣ 9876

♠ AK532
♡ 432
◇ 876
♣ 54

♠ 104
♡ QJ10
◇ 5432
♣ QJ102

♠ QJ8
♡ A865
◇ AKQ
♣ AK3

"I wonder," remarked the Emeritus Professor, offering the Hog his lighter, "how it is that North and South both happen to hold the eight of spades?"

"Kindly don't look," barked the Hideous Hog, hastily covering up the South and East hands with ashtrays. "You are West. After three passes South opens two no-trumps and North raises him to three no-trumps. You lead the three of spades to dummy's nine and partner's ten. Declarer wins with the knave and promptly returns the queen of spades. Go on from there."

Reluctantly, for he felt certain that a trap had been laid for him somewhere, the Emeritus Professor went up with the king of spades and continued with the ace.

"Declarer follows both times," said H.H. "Partner, who started with a doubleton, throws on the third round the two of diamonds."

The Professor continued with the five of spades.

"Partner discards the three of diamonds and declarer the five of hearts. Go on," urged the Hog.

S.B. took stock. Then it seemed as if the scales suddenly fell from his eyes and a purring note mingled with the customary hiss. "I lead the eight of diamonds," he breathed softly.

"Why?" asked H.H.

"Because," explained S.B., "my last spade would squeeze partner in hearts and clubs. Obviously declarer wouldn't have thrown spades back at me if he had nine tricks. No doubt his idea was to induce a suicide squeeze and partner's discards show that diamonds are not involved. Ergo I lead one." With a triumphant glint behind the pince-nez S.B. added: "I expect that you did the same, my dear H.H., but please note that you are not the only genius in these parts and that fanfare of trumpets ..."

A burst of laughter drowned the rest of the sentence. "I knew he'd fall for it," cried the Hideous Hog, "that is, after I'd made him take a good look at my hand – inadvertently, of course, while he lit my cigarette. Ha! Ha! As you can see," went on H.H. removing the ashtrays "the fifth spade would indeed be fatal to the defence. For the moment East can let go a third diamond, but when the ◊ A K Q are cashed he must come down to five cards and he needs six, for unless he keeps three clubs, the three of clubs will be South's ninth trick and if East parts with a heart, dummy's nine of hearts will be a winner. Only ... Ha! Ha! Ha! ..."

"What's so funny?" hissed S.B. angrily. "I beat the contract, didn't I?"

"Certainly you did," replied the Hog still shaking with laughter. "Only declarer didn't have the hand you think he had, the one you peeped at. I was declarer and Papa had your hand. He didn't see my cards as you did, of course, but he visualised my supposed holding from my play. Let me be the first to admit that you both defended very well – against the hand I palmed on you, so to speak."

Wiping the tears from his eyes, the Hog continued: "I could rely on Papa, who would be a fine player if he weren't so clever, to deduce my hand from my play. In your case, Professor, I thought that a little assistance such as a glimpse of my pseudo-hand, wouldn't be out of place. The result was the same. You both reasoned, as intended, that I wouldn't have led back a spade unless I wanted you to play off your spades. Therefore, to thwart me, you didn't – which was the only way I could stop you doing it. Shall we call it a little psychological confidence trick? I conjure up the spurious threat of a suicide squeeze to make you commit suicide!" Chortling happily, the Hog filled in the real holdings of South and East. He even altered one of the spade eights to a seven.

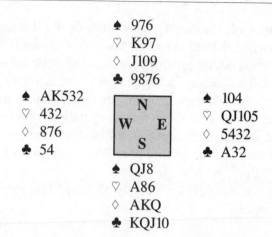

♠ 976
♡ K97
◊ J109
♣ 9876

♠ AK532
♡ 432
◊ 876
♣ 54

♠ 104
♡ QJ105
◊ 5432
♣ A32

♠ QJ8
♡ A86
◊ AKQ
♣ KQJ10

"Simple, isn't it ?" went on the Hog. "If the spades break four-four, I can't lose and if they are five-three I can't win. That's what it looks like at trick one. It struck me, though, that there might be a little misunderstanding if, as seemed likely enough, the ace of clubs was not in the hand with the spades. West wouldn't know that East had an ace and East wouldn't know that West had four winners, and if he didn't, he wouldn't start in time a delicate high-low signal in clubs.

"That gave me an idea. If I made Papa a Greek gift, a clever, imaginative player like Themistocles would wonder what was behind it and of course he would think of a suicide squeeze. Well, you know the rest. Rather neat, don't you think?" concluded the Hog, beaming happily.

"Neat!" repeated S.B. indignantly, "Brazenly forging a hand and obtaining my opinion under false pretences. Why, if we'd been talking for money I'd sue him. I'd ..."

Sleight of Hand
The Hideous Hog wasn't listening. He rarely did. Tearing down another notice from the board, an appeal for some worthy cause, he was scribbling busily.

"Sleight of hand is a technique," he said as he filled in the hands of North and East," just like squeezes or card-reading. We all know the mechanics of the safety play and of its counterpart – enlightened wishful thinking. When we have tricks to burn we think of the worst possible distribution, and when we are in a tough spot, we visualise a set-up in which every card is where we want it. Sometimes, though, even that isn't enough. Then we extend the principle and rely on friendship and co-operation from opponents. To deserve it, we must, of course, propitiate them and the best way is to present them with a picture of our hand, the sort of hand we want them to think we have."

Carefully replacing Walter's empty glass, the Hog passed round the charity appeal.

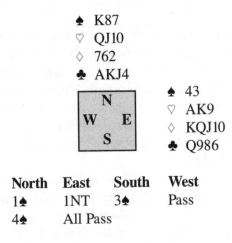

```
            ♠  K87
            ♡  QJ10
            ◇  762
            ♣  AKJ4
                          ♠  43
         ┌─────────┐      ♡  AK9
         │    N    │      ◇  KQJ10
         │  W   E  │      ♣  Q986
         │    S    │
         └─────────┘
```

North	East	South	West
1♣	1NT	3♠	Pass
4♠	All Pass		

"Now then, Oscar," went on the Hog. "You are East. Partner leads the ace of spades, then the two. Declarer wins in his hand and leads a club. West follows with the three of clubs and the ace goes up from the table. I want you to call the cards you play from now on."

"The six of clubs," announced O.O.

"The four of clubs is played next," said H.H.

The Owl paused. The eight of clubs was the obvious card to play, but there was bound to be a catch somewhere; only one didn't know where or when and one could be made to look foolish either way.

"Well," he mused aloud, "the two of clubs is missing, so

presumably partner is signalling. This he would do with an even number of clubs, two or four. If it's a doubleton, declarer has three, in which case his play makes no sense for his only chance is a successful finesse. Conversely, if Partner has four clubs, South has a singleton and intends to ruff a club in the hope that the queen will come down next time. That, at least, is consistent with the play." O.O. looked round for approval.

The Hog was writing down another hand and paid no attention.

"Could partner's club holding be 1073?" resumed Oscar. "That seems highly improbable for it leaves declarer with two, and if so, he would have nothing to gain by playing ace-small. No. He must have a singleton. Nothing else adds up. I play the eight of clubs."

The Hog unfolded the appeal to charity, showing us the full deal:

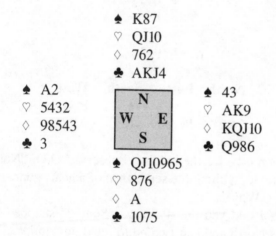

```
                ♠ K87
                ♡ QJ10
                ◊ 762
                ♣ AKJ4
  ♠ A2                        ♠ 43
  ♡ 5432        N             ♡ AK9
  ◊ 98543    W     E          ◊ KQJ10
  ♣ 3           S             ♣ Q986
                ♠ QJ10965
                ♡ 876
                ◊ A
                ♣ 1075
```

"You are quite right, Oscar," declared the Hog approvingly. "Declarer must have a singleton for nothing else adds up. Only declarer happened to be your humble servant and to enlist your co-operation I took the trouble to create the appropriate picture in your mind, to 'show' you my hand – at least the club part of it. I had nothing to lose, mind you, for your hand was marked with the queen of clubs on the bidding. The it-doesn't-add-up gambit gave me a chance to nothing, and that's always a good percentage play."

Superb Cunning

The Hog looked at the bottle. There was just time for another hand before dinner. "Now, Timothy," he said, "you shouldn't have much trouble with this one. Your friend the Rabbit was East. Papa, South, was declarer in four spades and trumps break two-two."

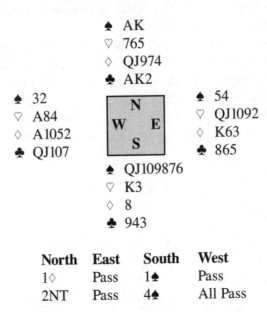

```
              ♠ AK
              ♡ 765
              ◇ QJ974
              ♣ AK2
  ♠ 32                      ♠ 54
  ♡ A84         N           ♡ QJ1092
  ◇ A1052    W     E        ◇ K63
  ♣ QJ107       S           ♣ 865
              ♠ QJ109876
              ♡ K3
              ◇ 8
              ♣ 943
```

North	East	South	West
1◇	Pass	1♠	Pass
2NT	Pass	4♠	All Pass

"I don't much care for the bidding," observed O.O. "North's two no-trumps rebid, without the semblance of a heart guard, is surely questionable. Why ..."

"Haven't I told you that Papa was South?" snapped back the Hog. "I was North and had I failed to rebid no-trumps at once, he would have got it in first to play the hand as he always does. No, no, the heart position was unfortunate, but it was a case of restricted choice – an indifferent bid or the risk that he would play the hand. Of course, I couldn't cope with a seven-card suit. But never mind the bidding. West opens the queen of clubs. Proceed."

The Toucan opened his mouth twice but said nothing.

"Seventeen," murmured Walter the Walrus, "and one more for the fifth diamond."

"I think the last hand gives us a clue to this one" said O.O. "I lead the four of diamonds from dummy, hoping that East has the ten. He's unlikely to cover and I lose the trick to West's ace or king. Then I set up a diamond, my tenth trick, by playing East for the other top honour. How's that?"

"Magnificent," replied H.H., uncovering the East/West hands, "only West happens to hold the ten of diamonds."

The Owl hooted softly.

"It's a good thing for you, really" went on H.H, "and you are in no trouble, for West can't lead a heart without throwing the contract at you. Say he leads another club. You win, throw your losing club on the queen of diamonds – unless East covers, of course – and you still set up a diamond."

"Is that how Papa played it?" asked T.T.

"Yes," replied the Hog.

"I hope that for once you said 'well played'," remarked Oscar.

"I don't regard it as good play to go down in a sitting contract," retorted H.H. heatedly.

"But how could he go down?" asked the Toucan, "you've just explained that he had ten tricks."

"And so he had," agreed the Hog, "but don't forget that Papa is superbly cunning, determined to deceive everyone with every card he plays. To trick one, the queen of clubs, captured in dummy, he followed from his own hand with the nine. It was meant to fool everyone. And so it did," went on the Hog bitterly, "the Rabbit, in particular, was completely taken in. He assumed, too, from the play that Papa had the ten of diamonds, and since he had apparently no club loser, the only hope for the defence was to set up two heart tricks before the diamonds were cleared. So the Rabbit went up gallantly with the king of diamonds on the first round and shot through the queen of hearts, and that was that.

"Oh, yes, Papa played the hand well, but he defended it better still. Can you wonder," concluded H.H., "that when I cut him I deviate sometimes from strict bidding orthodoxy with a view to locking him in dummy, as it were? He's such a good dummy."

Chapter Sixteen
Exhibition Bridge

"Take Plato, Socrates or even Aristotle. Take me."

Themistocles Papadopoulos was in an exuberant mood. We were drinking coffee on the terrace at the Unicorn, after dining with the Rueful Rabbit, and Papa was developing the thesis that every sage has a duty to pass on his wisdom to posterity. It was a sacred debt to the future which his forebears in ancient Greece had discharged in the realms of philosophy, politics and natural science. His own modest contribution would be in the domain of cards. A different medium but the same lofty principle.

The subject arose because Papa had invited his nephew, Sophocles, to join us at the Unicorn for a demonstration of high-class bridge. Sopho had been selected to play for his school against Eton and Papa had been coaching him intensively for weeks past.

"Tonight," declared the Greek, "I want my nephew to see the real thing, everything, yes, even the faults, the frailties, the follies, the futilities, the ..."

"Would you like him to sit beside me?" suggested the ever-helpful Rabbit.

"I said *everything*," went on Papa, with a pitying look at the Rabbit, "the howlers and the horrors, certainly, but also and above all, I want him to see how masters play, their brilliance in anticipation, their subtlety in deception, their flawless execution, their perfect ..."

"Oh! I see," broke in R.R., "you want your nephew to watch the Hideous Hog. You are absolutely right. Yes, of course, he should sit behind the Hog and I am sure H.H. won't mind."

Rising sharply, the Greek's eyebrows oscillated between anger and incredulity. The Hog indeed! Could it be that those chocolate and almond biscuits, which he was nibbling so assiduously, had gone to the poor Rabbit's head?

"Sophocles will sit by my side," announced Papa. Then, turning to me and dipping his gold-tipped cigarette in my coffee, he went on in softer tones: "You understand Greek, I know, but do you suppose the others will mind if I make an occasional remark to my nephew in our language? I would like to impress on him the finer points of the game as we go along." The Hideous Hog, who now joined us, was unusually accommodating.

"Of course, of course," he assured Papa eagerly, "pass on the secrets of your magic. Let this be an exhibition game which Polycrates – or is it Xerxes? – will remember for years to come. And if you like," he added invitingly, "we'll raise the stakes, just to give him an added interest. How about it?"

As we approached the card room, we heard a deep, resonant voice proclaim: "I had twenty." Walter the Walrus was explaining why he had been obliged to concede an 800 penalty.

Sophocles was slim and dark and sallow. He was visibly awed by his surroundings and treated Papa with all the respect to which he was unaccustomed.

The Hog cut an ace, the Greek a three. Walter and the Rabbit both drew the seven of spades. Trying again, this time from the same pack, R.R. cut a ten and faced the Hog.

Sophocles seated himself by my side between his uncle and the Rueful Rabbit.

Huit à la Banque

This was what we could see of the first deal:

Love All. Dealer West.

	N		♠ 8432
W		E	♡ 987
	S		◊ K10983
			♣ 2

♠ AQ976
♡ 32
◊ A2
♣ K984

West	North	East	South
H.H.	*W. W.*	*R.R.*	*Papa*
1◊	1♡	2◊	2♠
3NT	All Pass		

While the Walrus was debating what to lead, Papa whispered in Greek to his nephew: "You are wondering, of course, why I didn't double. The reason is twofold. First, a weak partner should never be trusted. Secondly, a strong opponent should be distrusted even more. Had I doubled, the Hog would have stepped smartly into four diamonds and with a weakling opposite it wouldn't be safe to double that. So let this be your first lesson of the evening. Take a certain profit. Never be greedy."

By this time the Walrus had decided to lead the five of spades. As dummy came into view Papa leant across me once more to whisper to Sophocles.

"The nine is the card to play. If the five is a singleton, I want to retain control till I can see what is going on. And if the Hog is spoofing, which is so often the case, the five may even turn out to be a true card – the fourth highest, you know – and it will then hold the trick. Either way the nine cannot lose."

The Hog captured the nine with the knave and attacked the diamonds. Coming in with the ace, the Greek decided to clear up the spade position without further ado. On the ace H.H. threw a small club. An anguished grimace from Papa matched a splutter of

impotent rage from the Walrus as it became apparent to both that
the Hideous Hog had stolen a vital trick with the singleton knave.
With a tchff, tchff, tchff-like noise, expressive of fury and
frustration, Walter the Walrus tugged first at the king, then at the
ten. Dummy's eight of spades leered at him mockingly for the suit
was well and truly blocked. This was the full deal:

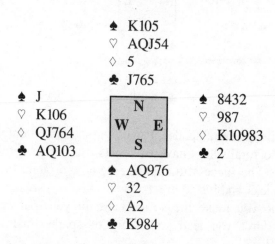

```
                      ♠ K105
                      ♡ AQJ54
                      ◇ 5
                      ♣ J765
     ♠ J                            ♠ 8432
     ♡ K106          N              ♡ 987
     ◇ QJ764      W     E           ◇ K10983
     ♣ AQ103         S              ♣ 2
                      ♠ AQ976
                      ♡ 32
                      ◇ A2
                      ♣ K984
```

Papa could still have won fame and glory by switching to a heart,
but that would have meant effacing himself, hardly the way to
impress a high-spirited nephew who had come to watch, to learn
and to admire. With a look of disgust he led a small spade on which
the Hog shed a heart.

Still spluttering incoherently and whispering dark imprecations
across the room, the Walrus banged the ace of hearts on the table,
then the queen. The Hog grabbed the trick with his king and set
forth on the diamonds, grunting voluptuously as his opponents
squirmed. With four cards left the position was:

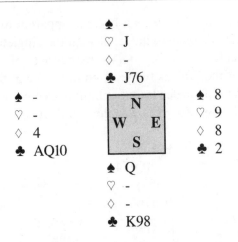

Guarding his queen of spades, Papa let go a club on dummy's last diamond. To retain his knave of hearts, the Walrus, too, parted with a club. The successful club finesse now brought the Hog the last three tricks and his contract.

"Why do you make life so difficult for your partner?" cried Papa. "Couldn't you lead your king of spades instead of the ridiculous five?"

"Only on Tuesday," countered the exasperated Walrus, "you insisted that from three to an honour the correct lead is the lowest. Why should it be so different on a Friday?"

"But then you ..."

"Tchff, tchff, tchff," angrily retorted W.W., closing the argument.

"Curious hand," observed Oscar the Owl, "though H.H. has made three no-trumps, five no-trumps by the other side cannot be broken."

"Or five hearts," put in Peregrine the Penguin.

"Or for that matter, five spades," ventured one of the lesser kibitzers.

"And why not six spades?" asked H.H., never loth to rub a little salt into Papa's wounds. "That is, double dummy, of course, the way your uncle plays every hand," he added with a wink at Sophocles.

"Assume the natural lead of a diamond. Declarer wins and ruffs a second diamond with dummy's ten of spades. Then he overtakes the king of trumps with the ace and takes the heart finesse. Next comes dummy's five of trumps and a finesse against the eight. Now the trumps are drawn and a second heart finesse clears that suit, yielding all told, five hearts, five trumps, the ace of diamonds and a diamond ruff concluded H.H., beaming at Papa.

"What do you think of it?" asked the Rabbit, turning to Sophocles.

"I still can't see why uncle did not double," replied the boy.

"No, no," broke in the Hideous Hog. "You must be fair. If your uncle intended to defend as he did, he was perfectly right not to double. Ha! Ha!"

"How many points did you have?" asked the Walrus, looking at the Hog suspiciously.

To Walter the Walrus, making tricks without points was like making bricks without straw, a shady practice, which might yield an occasional profit, but was bad bridge and savoured of immorality.

Fate Makes Amends

Papa sat back in his chair with the air of a righteous man who had been dealt the sort of hand he deserves. Perhaps Fate was trying to make amends – at long last. As I went to press the bell for the steward I glanced at all four hands:

East/West Game. Dealer South.

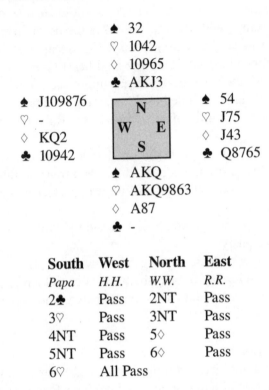

```
                    ♠ 32
                    ♡ 1042
                    ◊ 10965
                    ♣ AKJ3
    ♠ J109876              ♠ 54
    ♡ -          N         ♡ J75
    ◊ KQ2      W   E       ◊ J43
    ♣ 10942        S       ♣ Q8765
                    ♠ AKQ
                    ♡ AKQ9863
                    ◊ A87
                    ♣ -
```

South	West	North	East
Papa	*H.H.*	*W.W.*	*R.R.*
2♣	Pass	2NT	Pass
3♡	Pass	3NT	Pass
4NT	Pass	5◊	Pass
5NT	Pass	6◊	Pass
6♡	All Pass		

The Rabbit, whose thoughts had been wandering, asked to review the bidding. "Later," said the Hog, leading out the knave of spades.

Scowling at dummy, Papa spoke rapidly in Greek to his nephew: "In ancient Sparta imbeciles were destroyed at birth. The routine was to hurl them to destruction from a high cliff. These days they grow up in luxury and you may cut any one of them as your partner, like this one." Papa was still talking as he played to the first trick. "Of course, as you can see, Sopho," he went on, "fourteen tricks are cold, fourteen on a squeeze."

The ace of spades won the first trick and the ace of trumps followed. When H.H. showed out the Greek paused, frowned and lit a second cigarette. I moved away my coffee cup. After a while, he assumed a cunning look and led the king of spades, then the queen. The Rabbit, distrait as ever, threw a small club. Papa glared at him and Oscar the Owl nearly blinked. The Rueful Rabbit did not notice it. His thoughts were far away.

Muttering some Delphic oath under his breath, the Greek played the nine of hearts away from his king-queen, gently pushing the trick towards the Rabbit.

The knave was already in mid air, ready to drop on the proffered gift. Before it could reach the table, however, the Rabbit suddenly stopped in his tracks. The vibrations of his long, sensitive nose, the twitching of his left ear, the soft gurgle which came from the back of his throat, all proclaimed a desperate inner struggle. Slowly the knave sank back whence it came and with tremulous fingers the Rabbit played the seven of hearts. The Greek's offer of a trick was declined. The Rabbit looked around apprehensively, but all was well. Papa was in disarray and the Hog was wearing his most engaging sneer. Seconds later the contract was broken.

R.R.'s refusal first to ruff a spade, then to part prematurely with the knave of trumps, killed all Papa's hopes of entering dummy and reaching the two top clubs, and without them there was no way of avoiding two diamond losers.

"A brilliant defence," I heard one young Unicorn whisper. "How could he tell at the third trick that declarer had no club?"

Sophocles was deeply impressed. "Do you not think, uncle," he asked, "that I should sit behind that gentleman?"

Later that night, when we were on our way home together, I brought up the hand and I put it to the Rabbit that he probably didn't know at the time what trumps were.

"It wasn't quite that," he replied. "Of course, the bidding was very confusing with both of them calling no-trumps, but I did think that hearts were trumps until Papa did not draw them, if you see what I mean. When he went on playing spades, well, that did take me in. I thought if he doesn't draw trumps, it can only be because there aren't any."

"But didn't the scales fall from your eyes when Papa led the nine of hearts, offering you a trick out of the blue?" I persisted.

"Oh yes, I knew then," R.R. assured me confidently.

"Then why did you duck it?"

"Well," explained the Rabbit, "I reasoned that if Papa offered me a trick, it could only be because it was in his interest that I should take it. So it was in mine not to. If you trust your opponent, do the opposite of anything he wants. There's no need to go into it too deeply, is there?" And as an afterthought, he added: "That nine of Papa's, it's what's known as a Greek gift, isn't it?"

A Ghoulash

Papa made game, then a partscore of 30. Next came a throw-in and according to the usual practice at the Unicorn it was to be followed by a goulash. In a goulash, the cards, unshuffled, are dealt five at a time to each player, then, on the third round, in threes. This leads to exotic distributions and often to the wildest bidding.

"You look hot," said Papa, unexpectedly, to the Walrus.

"What? Me? Hot?" boomed Walter, taken aback by such unaccustomed solicitude.

"Yes. Let's change places. The light on this side is much better, too," said the Greek ingratiatingly, moving out of his seat. Leaning over to his nephew, he whispered: "Tactics. A goulash has the effect of bumping up the stakes and I want to sit over the Hog." There was a greedy glint in the Hog's eye, but he said nothing.

The Walrus, now sitting South, dealt and opened three hearts.

Sophocles and I had moved with Papa and as before we could see his hand and the Rabbit's.

Game All. North/South 30. Dealer South.

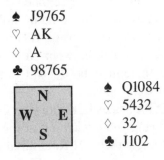

South	West	North	East
W.W.	*H.H.*	*Papa*	*R.R.*
3♡	4♣	4♡	Pass
Pass	4♠	Dble	Pass
5◇	Pass	6♡	6♠
Pass	Pass	7♡	Pass
Pass	7♠	Dble	All Pass

Papa's jump to six hearts was understandable enough for, by removing the double of four spades, the Walrus revealed a red two-suiter with, at most, one outside loser. The Rabbit's bid of six spades surprised me, but again a case could be made for it. If H.H. was willing, unaided, to sacrifice against a game, R.R. couldn't be blamed unduly for sacrificing against a slam.

The big surprise was Papa's call of seven hearts. It was a Master Bid, as he was the first to admit, and he promptly explained the reasons to Sophocles. "Of course, I have the double of the century. Anyone can see that. But you should always learn to look ahead, my boy. If opponents are willing to pay the price for saving a small slam, they will be more willing still to stop a grand slam. It's simple arithmetic. In this case, I run no risk at all, for I have both red aces and they certainly cannot rely on taking a trick with a black one. So I simply double them in seven spades instead of being satisfied with a double of six spades."

And so it came to pass. The Hog duly bid seven spades, and as he doubled in a voice that would have done credit to the Walrus, Papa made no attempt to suppress a note of triumph which proclaimed a conqueror in the hour of victory.

Softly the Greek murmured to his nephew: "A trump is the classical lead to reduce possible ruffs, but there's a chance that partner has twelve red cards and one spade. If so, he can ruff a club. Meanwhile, my ace of diamonds won't run away. Neither, for that matter, will the ace-king of hearts."

Papa opened a club, which the Hog won with the ten on the table. The Walrus, glaring angrily, threw a diamond. That first trick just about pinpointed every card at the table and thereafter the

Hideous Hog played double dummy.

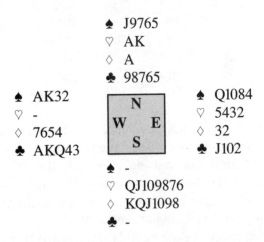

The Hog's main concern was to take tricks with his two and three of spades before Papa could discard a heart. To the second trick he led a heart from dummy and ruffed in his hand, then a club to the knave and another heart ruff. Now came the rest of the clubs on which two diamonds were discarded from dummy. With six cards left the position was:

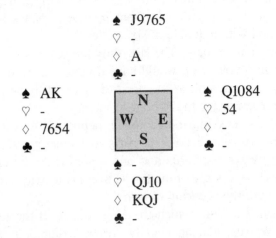

A diamond was ruffed on the table and with only trumps left the

Greek underruffed – or was overruffed – on each one of the last five tricks.

The Walrus spluttered indignantly. "What did you think I had on a three-bid?" he roared. "Double on your own hand, not on mine. I had nine points, too. I might have had much less. Tchff, tchff, tchff."

"Sorry, partner," jeered the Hog, "on that lead I should have made an overtrick. I played too quickly."

"Why did you lead a club?" bellowed Walter the Walrus. "Didn't you hear me bid two other suits?"

"What did you think of it?" the Rabbit asked Sophocles.

"I think," replied the boy, "that it would have been better tactics for uncle not to change seats."

Chapter Seventeen
The Horned Angel

Dinner was drawing to a close. With the empty magnum out of the way, Papa laid on the table a cutting from the evening paper. "Those dreary problems!" he said scornfully. "South to make ten tricks against the best defence," he read out. "The best indeed! That's the sort of thing for your dehydrated computer. At the table the human factor, the inhuman if you like, predominates. The best declarer rarely allows the best defence, and yet he may be floored by the worst, precisely because it is so bad that he cannot foresee it."

"If you are thinking of the Rabbit," began someone, but no one was listening. We all had stories to tell and looked around for bits of paper, all, that is, except the Hog, who had cornered the nutcrackers and was concentrating on the Taylor '55.

"Talking of the best defence," began Oscar the Owl, "I must tell you of a hand ..."

"I saw a curious example of defensive play only yesterday," interjected Peregrine the Penguin, casting his eyes around for something to write on.

Possession being nine-tenths of the law, I was holding on firmly to the wine list. Under the liqueurs there was ample room for a diagram. "I think," I said, "that you would like to hear about my hand. It illustrates Papa's point to perfection."

Papa grimaced as he recognised the hand. "Silly story. Now let me show you ..." But he, too, could find nothing to write on and gave way with a growl before my display of power politics.

Playing to the Score

This was my hand:

Game All. Dealer South.

S.B.
♠ J2
♡ J2
◊ AKQ10
♣ AK432

```
    N
  W   E
    S
```

Papa
♠ A543
♡ AQ83
◊ J987
♣ 5

South	West	North	East
		1♣	Pass
1◊	Pass	3◊	Pass
3♡	Pass	5◊	All Pass

As the Rabbit led the king of spades I saw Papa look attentively at the running total of the score, which was clearly inscribed at the top of his 'We' column. The figure was 120. The contract was, of course, unbeatable, but if Papa made all thirteen tricks, the rubber would come to 760 and that 60 would be worth an extra point to his side.

Was it possible to make all the tricks? Yes, there was just a chance for a superb technician like Papa and he seized it with alacrity. His plan consisted of setting up a long club in dummy, and in combining a dummy reversal with a variation on the guard squeeze theme. If the king of hearts was with Walter the Walrus, who was sitting East, and the Rueful Rabbit had the ten and nine, he would be squeezed, in the majors in the three-card ending. The position would be:

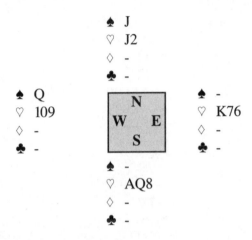

The heart finesse would now bring in the remaining three tricks.

Having made his dispositions, the Greek did not falter. Winning the first trick with the ace of spades, he led a club to dummy, ruffed a club, entered dummy with a trump, ruffed a second club and once more crossed to the table with a diamond. Now he drew trumps. Dummy had two more than were left in the closed hand and Papa got rid of two of his little spades. The fourth spade and the three of hearts were parked on the last two clubs, the king and the two, and the stage was set for a guard squeeze.

While Papa was flashing card after card, looking significantly at the kibitzers to make sure that his artistry was not wasted, R.R.'s long sensitive nose was twitching nervously, a sure sign of tension and excitement. He, too, had learned the technique of keeping a running total of the score and in his 'They' column he had noted a difference of 140, which meant that Papa would need 120, twelve tricks, to earn to extra point.

The Rabbit had never excelled at arithmetic, but it was clear to him from the start that come what may, he must never allow himself to be thrown in with the queen of spades and so forced to lead a heart away from his king, for that would present Papa with his twelfth, decisive trick, while it could make no difference to the score whether he made twelve tricks or thirteen.

When three cards were left, the Greek led triumphantly dummy's knave of hearts. Since East did not cover, he ran it and the astounded Rabbit, who had bared his king to avoid the endplay, could not help winning the last three tricks.

This was the full deal:

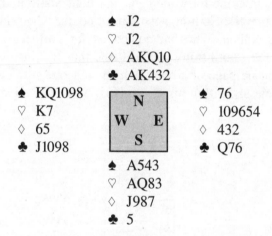

```
              ♠ J2
              ♡ J2
              ◇ AKQ10
              ♣ AK432
  ♠ KQ1098                 ♠ 76
  ♡ K7          N          ♡ 109654
  ◇ 65       W     E       ◇ 432
  ♣ J1098       S          ♣ Q76
              ♠ A543
              ♡ AQ83
              ◇ J987
              ♣ 5
```

Papa's luckless brilliance brought cries of rage from his partner, the Emeritus Professor of Bio-Sophistry.

The Greek hastened to explain that the odds against finding the Rabbit with the bare king of hearts were positively astronomical, while the extra point for the rubber was not to be sneezed at. In the long run such things made quite a difference.

"Which extra points?" hissed S.B. angrily.

"The difference being 120 ..." began the Greek.

"No, 140, surely ..." corrected the Rabbit.

"The difference in the totals was precisely 110," announced the Emeritus Professor. "If you must keep the aggregate, hand by hand, I suggest that in fairness to your partners you should use an abacus." That evidently gave R.R. an idea and I saw him surreptitiously tying a knot in his handkerchief.

Having told my story, I handed the wine list over to the Owl.

Papa was about to say something, but all the nuts had gone and the Hideous Hog could be denied no longer.

Do Your Worst

"What none of you seem to realise," he declared, twirling his empty glass with a meaningful look at the Penguin, "is that there's an answer to the worst defence. The worst dummy play can be just as effective. Imagine for a moment that both South and East are truly lethal players. Nothing personal, of course," he said, turning towards the Rabbit, who had joined us for coffee a couple of minutes earlier, "but I think you will find this deal instructive."

On the inside page of a book, which someone at the next table had left carelessly within his reach, H.H. wrote down two hands.

♠ AKJ32
♡ K2
♢ A32
♣ A32

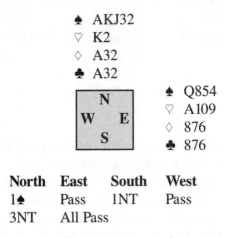

♠ Q854
♡ A109
♢ 876
♣ 876

North	East	South	West
1♠	Pass	1NT	Pass
3NT	All Pass		

"West opens the six of hearts. Got it? Very well. What should East do if declarer plays low from dummy? He finds the nine? Naturally. Anyone can see that – well, almost anyone," added H.H., with a malicious look at the Rabbit. "But now look at the full deal:

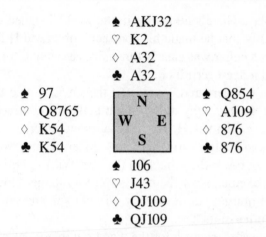

♠ AKJ32
♡ K2
◇ A32
♣ A32

♠ 97
♡ Q8765
◇ K54
♣ K54

♠ Q854
♡ A109
◇ 876
♣ 876

♠ 106
♡ J43
◇ QJ109
♣ QJ109

"As you can see," went on H.H., "if all play intelligently, declarer is home. He plays the two from dummy and takes East's nine with the knave. Now, since the finesse and 3-3 split in spades would only yield eight tricks, he tries first one minor, then the other. He can't lose. If, however, East, knowing no better, goes up with the ace of hearts on the two and returns another heart, declarer, locked in dummy, is helpless. The unthinking defence wins in a canter."

"Just my point," interposed Papa.

Barely pausing for a malevolent glance, the Hog continued: "And now observe how easily the worst dummy play circumvents the worst defence. Not realising that by playing low from dummy he can stop the suit, regardless of the position of the cards, declarer thinks he is on a guess and goes up with the king. This atrocious play pays handsomely. East wins and returns the ten. But South covers and the suit is blocked. Whether West ducks or wins, continues with hearts or switches, the defence can only come to four tricks – three hearts and one other trick, maybe a spade."

"I remember the hand well," murmured Papa uneasily.

"Surely," said the Penguin incredulously, "no declarer in real life was bad enough to go up with the king?"

"Oh yes," answered the Hog, "declarer happened to be Walter the Walrus, who is bad enough for anything."

"To think that a player should make his contract through such abominable play. There's no justice in the world," sighed Oscar.

"I did not say that he made his contract," observed H.H.

The Rabbit's collar was clearly three sizes too small for him and he had turned a deep vermilion.

"But I don't understand," persisted the Owl, "Since the heart suit was now blocked, why didn't South make his contract?"

"Because," explained H.H., "East was none other than our friend, R.R., and contrary to what many lesser players would have done, he did not cover the king with the ace. With lightning speed he produced the nine. Now the hearts were no longer blocked and declarer could not get out of dummy without surrendering a trick in one of the other suits."

Was that another triumph for the worst defence or was the hold up of the ace a master stroke? And if so, how did the Rueful Rabbit come to perpetrate it?

In a sense, it was all a question of timing. I watched the hand and I remember how long the Walrus meditated before playing to the first trick. Where was the ace? Where was the queen? It seemed to him to be a blind guess and as he debated the issue the minutes slipped by.

The Rabbit, growing restless and fidgeting as was his wont, detached the nine from his hand, fully expecting the Walrus to play dummy's two of hearts. "They usually do," he explained apologetically afterwards.

When, at last, the king appeared from dummy he released the nine automatically from his hand. As it fell, he gave an anguished cry, but it was too late. The Rabbit had played the wrong card and broken the contract.

"It was an outrage," cried Papa. "Even I could do nothing to stop it. I was dummy."

"You must not blame yourself," observed Oscar the Owl philosophically. "It was just R.R.'s guardian angel."

"That angel," fumed Papa, "has horns and a long vicious tail!"

A popping cork interrupted the conversation. When it was resumed, a couple of glasses later, Papa, who had been thinking hard, was the first to speak.

Chapter Eighteen
The Possessed

Slowly the Greek stretched his hand for *The Possessed*, the book which H.H. had grabbed to write down his hand. "Having paid tribute to the worst dummy play and the worst defence, how about a triumph for the worst bidding?" Papa looked scornfully at the Hog. "There you are. You go first, Oscar. How do you bid these hands?"

On the title page, under Fyodor Dostoyevsky, Papa presented this diagram:

Game All. Dealer South.

♠ KQJ2
♡ J9
◇ J
♣ AQJ1098

♠ A1087
♡ Q1087
◇ AK10
♣ K6

"Rubber bridge or duplicate?" enquired Peregrine the Penguin.

"Either or both," replied the Greek, "but as it happens the deal occurred in a pairs event, quite recently, too."

"Well," began Oscar, "North forces with three clubs over South's opening one spade and South rebids three hearts. I prefer that to three no-trumps in case there's a four-four fit which might otherwise be lost."

Peregrine nodded solemnly in acquiescence and took up the bidding sequence. "North jumps to four spades to show exceptional trump support and South invites a slam with a bid of five diamonds. North, however, has no more to say and signs off in five spades which becomes the final contract."

"Not too difficult a problem," observed O.O.

"Any good pair should reach the par contract of five spades," agreed P.P.

"Then," cried the Hog, waving someone's cigar, "allow me to inform you that par is an ass, an ignoramus, a moujhik, for your five spades isn't worth the diagram it's scribbled on."

"Surely ..." began Oscar.

With an unmistakable gesture, H.H. brushed him aside. "In a duplicate pairs event, which this was, some Souths would probably open one no-trump and some Norths, disdaining Stayman at matchpoint scoring, would raise to three no-trumps, and, as there are no more losers in no-trumps than in spades, your famous par would be an also-ran. Other pairs would doubtless reach a slam and so should you, of course."

"With two top losers?" asked P.P. incredulously.

"You've forgotten your own bidding," retorted H.H. "After that rebid of three hearts, no West is likely to open the suit unless he holds the ace-king. He might lead a heart from ace-doubleton against five spades, hoping for a ruff should partner come to life with an early entry, and he would find it, too, of course, since East has the king of hearts. Give North an extra heart, instead of a diamond, and five spades could go down where six spades would be a make. But that's by the way. The point is that you want to be in a slam on a finesse ..."

"Which finesse?" asked someone.

"I mean a fifty-fifty chance. Same thing," replied the Hog. "Without a heart lead you have twelve tricks on top. And you have a better than fifty-fifty chance that West will not open a heart. In short, the slam is a good one, and the par contract is a bad one."

"So declarer bids six spades," said O.O., "and West doesn't lead a heart."

"Well, it wasn't quite like that," interjected the Hog. "I, er, that is partner ..."

"He did far worse," cried Papa, "he bid seven spades, yes, seven! Oh, yes, he was South and he has the effrontery to defend it!"

H.H. put down my glass. "As you all know," he began, "I'm no result merchant. I never cover up mistakes and I admit frankly that my partner overbid his hand grossly. Up to five diamonds our sequence was the same as yours, Oscar. But then, instead of signing off in five spades, as he should have done, he called six clubs. Of course I bid seven spades. Naturally. But I do not claim that it was the best contract, only that seven spades, though inferior to six spades, was better than your fatuous, silly double dummy par of five spades."

Wagging a fat, pink forefinger, the Hideous Hog concluded: "At duplicate pairs par allows you to share a bottom. The grand slam makes the bottom more frigid if it fails, but gains an undisputed top when it succeeds, that is when the ace of hearts is with East, which will happen half the time. At rubber bridge or in a match, you risk the loss of a game and stand to gain 750 or 1500 points, and again it's an even money chance. So much for par."

East v. West

"There is one situation we haven't covered," I suggested. "We have seen some curious twists in the perennial struggle between declarer and the defence, but what of the duel, no less deadly at times, between East and West?"

The waiter had brought the bill. There was no wild scramble to seize it, so I could set out on the back, at my leisure, a deal to illustrate my theme. As I started to jot down West's hand Papa winced, looked anxiously at his watch and announced: "It's later than I think. I have an urgent appointment." And with that he made a hasty exit.

"We must all suffer in life," observed the Hog philosophically, "but it's too much to ask anyone to have the same tooth extracted twice." The Hog had enjoyed, as dummy, this deal which had come up a few days earlier:

North/South Game. Dealer South.

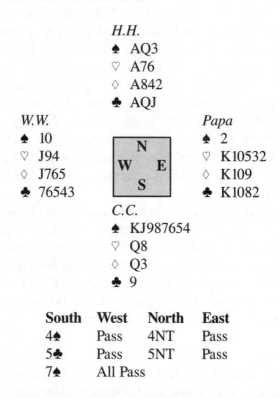

```
                        H.H.
                        ♠ AQ3
                        ♡ A76
                        ◇ A842
                        ♣ AQJ
     W.W.                                    Papa
     ♠ 10               ┌─────────┐          ♠ 2
     ♡ J94              │    N    │          ♡ K10532
     ◇ J765            W│         │E         ◇ K109
     ♣ 76543            │    S    │          ♣ K1082
                        └─────────┘
                        C.C.
                        ♠ KJ987654
                        ♡ Q8
                        ◇ Q3
                        ♣ 9
```

South	West	North	East
4♠	Pass	4NT	Pass
5♣	Pass	5NT	Pass
7♠	All Pass		

Colin the Corgi, who was the Hog's partner, was a little unlucky, I thought, to find dummy with two queens and a knave that were useless, instead of either red king, which would have made the grand slam a laydown.

The Corgi won the opening trump lead in dummy and played off the two red aces before reeling off the spades. His intentions were unmistakable. The club finesse had to be right, but since it couldn't be repeated he was engineering a double Vienna Coup to improve his chances. If Walter the Walrus, sitting West, had a red king as well as the king of clubs, he would be inexorably squeezed in the three-card ending.

As any competent kibitzer could tell at a glance, the Walrus was in no danger, but Papa, having all three kings, would be caught in a progressive squeeze from which there could be no escape. The Greek saw it in a flash, and playing as if he hadn't a care in the world, smoothly bared his three kings. The order of his discards was instructive. Parting with the two of clubs, the eight of clubs and the ten of clubs in the early stages, he gave declarer no inkling of his dire predicament. The Walrus puffed and panted as was his wont. Resenting a high-speed game, he glowered at Papa and the Corgi, in turn, to show them that he wouldn't be rushed.

The Corgi's last three cards were a club and the two red queens. Dummy retained the ace-queen-knave of clubs, while Papa sat over it with three unguarded kings, fated, it seemed, to score all three.

When Colin led his eighth spade, the Walrus shed his last club, leaving himself with the knave-nine of hearts and the knave of diamonds. I don't know how carefully the Corgi had counted the discards, for they could hardly affect his plan of campaign, but when he finally led a club and W.W. showed out, it was all over. The ace brought down the lone king and it only remained to add up the score.

"Saboteur! Quisling!" cried Papa. "Why out of your thirteen useless cards couldn't you keep a club?"

"He only had small ones," interjected Colin, winking at the kibitzers.

"Don't blame me," protested the Walrus indignantly. "I had two points and I kept them both to the end. Had *you* kept a small club, instead of trying to be clever, your king wouldn't have dropped ..."

Roars of rage from Papa and a burst of laughter from the Corgi and the Hog drowned the rest of the sentence.

T.T. Demotes a Winner

"You need shed no tears for Papa," said the Hog, when I had finished my story. "He gets more than his fair share of support from the opposition."

Someone had removed *The Possessed* and H.H. was reduced to writing down his hand below mine, on the back of the bill.

Game All. Dealer East.

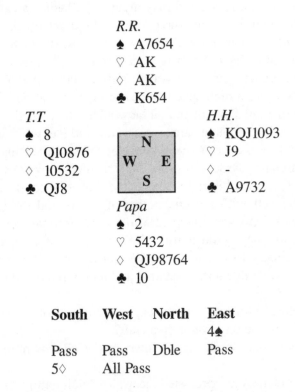

R.R.
♠ A7654
♡ AK
◇ AK
♣ K654

T.T.
♠ 8
♡ Q10876
◇ 10532
♣ QJ8

H.H.
♠ KQJ1093
♡ J9
◇ -
♣ A9732

Papa
♠ 2
♡ 5432
◇ QJ98764
♣ 10

South	West	North	East
			4♠
Pass	Pass	Dble	Pass
5◇	All Pass		

"There," he said. "The distribution is not inconsistent with the bidding, so play double dummy if you like. The eight of spades is led. Go on from there."

The Owl blinked sagely. The Penguin nodded in agreement. The Rabbit was the first to speak.

"You have ten top tricks and you score the eleventh by ruffing a heart in dummy. What's the problem?"

"And how do you get back to your hand to play the third heart?" asked the Hog.

"Simple," replied the Rabbit. "After cashing the ace-king of hearts I lead a club, I ruff the next one and ..."

"Meanwhile," pointed out H.H., "when East comes in with that club, he leads a spade. Unless you ruff high you'll be overruffed, and if you do, you'll later lose a trick to the ten. Papa allowed for that and sacrificed a trump trick in exchange for a second heart ruff in dummy. After the ace-king of hearts, he ruffed a spade high, ruffed a heart, came back with another high ruff and ruffed his last heart in dummy.

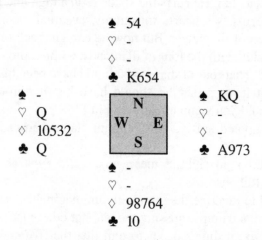

```
                      ♠ 54
                      ♡ -
                      ◊ -
                      ♣ K654
   ♠ -                              ♠ KQ
   ♡ Q          N                   ♡ -
   ◊ 10532   W      E               ◊ -
   ♣ Q          S                   ♣ A973
                      ♠ -
                      ♡ -
                      ◊ 98764
                      ♣ 10
```

"Now he played a low club and this is where we come to the climacteric, as Churchill would have said. I went up with the ace of clubs and shot another spade through the closed hand, forcing Papa to ruff high, thereby promoting the Toucan's five of diamonds. A pretty piece of work, you must admit."

"So you beat the contract after all?" said O.O.

"Of course I beat it," rejoined the Hog, "but my alleged partner promptly unbeat it. That Toucan, believe it or not, overruffed, yes, just like that. He wasn't prepared to sit there with 10-5-3-2, over the 8-7-6-4, and wait patiently for two tricks to fall into his lap.

Your Toucan talks glibly about smother plays and squeezes, and he can mix up any number of signals and conventions, but the basic, elementary mechanics of promotion are quite beyond him," concluded the Hog with an eloquent snort.

"Bad luck on you, of course," agreed the Penguin, "but Papa's good play did deserve a little luck."

"What!" cried the Hog. "You think that for butchering an unbeatable contract he deserved good luck?"

"Unbeatable?" repeated O.O. and P.P. in unison. "How?"

"R.R. showed you the way," replied the Hog, "Inadvertently, I admit, before he had given the matter any thought, but his instinct was right, just the same. To trick four, after the ace-king of hearts, declarer leads a club. He ruffs the spade return high and proceeds, as before, to ruff two hearts in dummy, eventually conceding a trick to the ten of diamonds. But now he can get back to his hand by ruffing a club with the four of diamonds, without promoting the Toucan's five. That four of diamonds should have been his eleventh trick. He lost it, or rather he should have lost it, through gross carelessness and you sympathise with him!"

The Owl hooted softly. The Penguin flapped impatiently his flippers.

"Where did I go right, I mean where did Papa go wrong?" enquired the Rabbit.

"He failed to imagine the seemingly unimaginable," replied the Hog. "With nine trumps, missing the ten, but otherwise solid right down to the six, it didn't occur to him that the five could live to take a trick against him by right of seniority. And so he neglected an elementary precaution. You'd be surprised how often contracts are lost that way."

The Radio-Active Rabbit

"When East and West are in contention," went on H.H., "the wrongdoer starts with a natural advantage and usually wins. And yet, at times, a defender can get the better of partner and declarer alike. Remember that hand which so incensed Papa the other day?"

"The radio-active hand?" I asked.

"That's the one," agreed the Hog, chortling gleefully as he recalled Papa's discomfiture. The Rabbit had left us, but not before ordering more port, and while the Hog gave it his undivided attention, I told the story to O.O. and P.P.

The Hog had the Rabbit as his partner. Papa had cut a polite, well-mannered young Griffin, but nothing else was remarkable about him and I forget his name. Before long this hand came up. I saw it played from a seat next to Papa.

Love All. Dealer South.

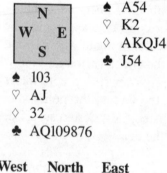

♠ A54
♡ K2
◊ AKQJ4
♣ J54

♠ 103
♡ AJ
◊ 32
♣ AQ109876

South	West	North	East
H.H.	*Papa*	*R.R.*	*P.Y.G.*
1♣	Pass	Pass	Dble
4♣	4♡	All Pass	

The Rabbit led the king of clubs, and while Papa surveyed the scene, I put myself in the Hog's place, wondering how he would plan the defence. With luck there would be two club tricks to pick up and, of course, the ace of trumps. What else? Spades offered little hope, for partner had passed one club and having shown up with a king in one suit was hardly likely to produce the king-knave in another. And nothing less would do, for as soon as declarer had cleared trumps he would park his losers on dummy's solid diamonds.

The only hope, then, was to collect two trump tricks. Was that possible? Papa could be credited with six hearts. Even so, the

Rabbit might have 10xx or 9xx. Even the eight would be promoted if the Greek had to ruff high twice.

Playing quickly and confidently, as was his custom, the Hog overtook the king of clubs with the ace and continued with the queen, Papa following. The first hurdle was over. A third club was ruffed by declarer with the ten, R.R. shedding spades both times. Next came the three of trumps to dummy's king. The Rabbit played the eight and the Hog, winning with the ace, again led a club.

The situation appeared to be perfectly straightforward and I couldn't imagine what Papa, his lips pursed, his eyes closed, could be thinking about. Either the Rabbit had the nine of hearts, in which case the contract was doomed, or Papa had the nine himself, and if so, he had nothing to worry about. Emerging finally from his deep trance, the Greek ruffed the club with the four of trumps. The Rabbit promptly over-ruffed with the five and it was all over.

The Hog, the Greek, the polite young Griffin and two Junior Kibitzers registered shock and surprise.

This was the deal:

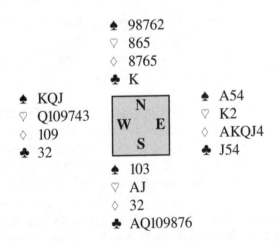

```
              ♠ 98762
              ♡ 865
              ◇ 8765
              ♣ K
  ♠ KQJ          N          ♠ A54
  ♡ Q109743   W     E       ♡ K2
  ◇ 109          S          ◇ AKQJ4
  ♣ 32                      ♣ J54
              ♠ 103
              ♡ AJ
              ◇ 32
              ♣ AQ109876
```

"Why did you recklessly throw away your eight of hearts, the only card in your hand that mattered?" enquired the Hog.

"I made the proper and correct signal to indicate three trumps and a desire to ruff," replied R.R. with simple dignity.

"Wasn't it a little careless on your part, sir, to ruff with the four?" asked the younger of the kibitzers, addressing Papa. "Couldn't you spare the seven?"

"Indeed he couldn't," replied the Hog, who was beginning to enjoy the situation. "But let me tell you first why Papa meditated so long and so deeply before plummeting to disaster. Believe it or not, he was working out a Grand Coup! Thinking, mistakenly, of course, that my partner knew what he was doing, he naturally assumed that his eight of hearts was a singleton. That left me with the ace-knave-six-five of hearts. I had shown up with seven clubs, so that I could only have two cards which weren't clubs or trumps. If both were diamonds, it could be done. Wasn't that what you were working out, Papa? You're among friends. Admit it."

Before the Greek could so much as splutter, H.H. was again in full flood. Card by card, he went over Papa's plan of campaign. After that second ruff, his trumps would be reduced to the same number as the Hog's, three each. He would cross to dummy with a diamond and lead a trump, taking the marked finesse. Going over to dummy again, assuming that H.H. had that second all-important diamond, he would lead diamonds, discarding spades, until the Hog was forced to ruff. Poised over the Hog's knave-six of hearts, he would be sitting with the queen-seven.

"You can see now," said the Hog to the young kibitzer, "why Papa couldn't afford the seven. He needed it for his coup."

"That Rabbit!" went on H.H. with a chuckle. "He ruins my defence, presents declarer with his contract and robs him of it in the same movement. His fall-out is deadly to all around him, partner, declarer and kibitzers alike. Why, he is positively radio-active."

I remembered the hand well.

The last of the port had slithered down the Hog's gullet. A far-away look came into his eyes. "Circumventing lethal partners poses some interesting problems, you know. Bidding their cards isn't too difficult. Playing them calls for a certain technique. I have been giving the matter a lot of thought lately."

Chapter Nineteen
From Each According to his Debility

"I deplore all this pseudo sportsmanship," declared the Hideous Hog, moodily twirling an empty glass. "It's undignified. One doesn't cheer at billiards when a player doesn't miscue or at tennis when someone gets the ball over the net. Why, then, should one pat partner on the back every time he counts correctly up to thirteen?"

"Because ..." began Oscar the Owl.

"Of course not," snapped the Hog indignantly. "Weaklings fawn on other weaklings because each one, in turn, hopes to be fawned upon himself. I find all this synthetic civility utterly sickening."

"You don't always practise what you preach, H.H." observed O.O., looking sceptical, as he recalled certain episodes in the campaign for the election of new members to the committee. "Why, you've been known to be civil yourself on occasion. Only yesterday you said, 'Well played, sir' to Timothy when he made four hearts on ..."

"Yes, yes," joined in the Rueful Rabbit eagerly, "I was at the table and I can tell you that Timothy was quite upset. He's not used to that sort of thing. After all, he was only doing his best, so why be sarcastic?"

"He played very well," insisted the Hog.

"But how do you know?" protested the Owl. "You didn't see the hand and it wasn't until someone called 'table up' that you came over from ..."

With a gesture of impatience, the Hog brushed this aside as

being strictly irrelevant.

"As you know," he declared, "that Toucan rarely makes as many as ten tricks, so he must have played well. 'Man bites dog' is news, as they say in Fleet Street, and 'Toucan makes tricks' is even bigger news, and when that happens he is entitled to a few words of praise."

O.O. shook his head. "Not for that hand," he said firmly. "There were twelve cold tricks on any lead, thirteen if he guessed correctly at the end that there were no more diamonds out."

"All the more reason for praising him," retorted the Hog warmly. "What if there were thirteen tricks about? Since he couldn't make more than ten, he showed excellent judgment by stopping in game. So not only did he play well, but he bid well, too, and what's more, owing to his, er, restraint, his precision bidding, the rubber was over and I could cut in. That's purely incidental, of course, but it's quite exasperating to be kept waiting by people who get into fatuous slams that can't get one anywhere anyway."

The Hog signalled to the barman. "I think this gentleman is trying to attract your attention," he told him, pointing to Colin the Corgi, who had just joined us. Then, having made sure of a refill, he pursued his lament on misguided sportsmanship.

"I am not against civility as such," he explained. "By all means give the devil his due, providing he deserves it. But it's up to every player to improve on the handicap imposed upon him by nature. What was it Marx said, or was it Gladstone? 'To each according to his needs, from each according to his debility.' That's it. Points should be awarded for surpassing oneself, for improving on nature, so to speak."

"But how would it work out in practice?" asked the Rabbit apprehensively. "For what would you award your points to, say, the Professor or to Charlie?"

Measuring Merit

"Quite simple," replied the Hog. "Your Secretary Bird would be doing well if he concentrated on the play instead of hissing and invoking the laws, as often as not to his disadvantage. We can't blame him for being a pest, of course, for such was nature's design, but if he became a lesser pest he would be deserving of praise. And so with Charlie the Chimp. Should he, at any time, attend to the hand he holds, instead of analysing the one before, he ought to be commended, for it doesn't come naturally to him to think of what he is doing. Papa is an even better example. One day he will see, perhaps, that though he cannot fool all the people all the time, he fools Papa most of the time. Not that the scales are ever likely to fall from his eyes," added the Hog.

"Do you mean," asked the Corgi, "that poor Papa has never done anything deserving of praise?"

"Yes, yes, he must have done," H.H. conceded the point without conviction. He was about to say something else, probably quite a lot, when suddenly he seemed to change his mind. A mischievous look came into the small beady eyes and, bringing out from his pocket a final demand for the rates, he began to scribble across the faint blue figures.

Playing with the Odds

"Now you come to mention it," he said softly, "Papa played a hand very well only the other day. There was another good hand in the same rubber, too. I'll show you both. Here you are. Papa is South with Karapet, the Free Armenian, as his partner. Don't worry about the bidding, for Papa was going to play the hand whatever happened, so it didn't matter much how he got there."

Love All. Dealer East.

♠ K43
♥ AKQ92
♦ J842
♣ 5

♠ A102
♥ J3
♦ 97
♣ AQJ963

South	West	North	East
			1♦
2♣	Pass	2♦	Pass
3♣	Pass	3♥	Pass
3NT	Pass	Pass	Pass

"The opening lead was the ten of diamonds, and on that lead," went on H.H., "no one could ask for a fairer contract. So let's make it. You go first, Oscar."

"I cover, naturally," said the Owl.

"East wins with the queen and switches to a spade. You play the ten of spades and take West's knave with the king. Agree? Then pray proceed."

"I take the club finesse," said O.O.

"The queen holds. What next?" enquired H.H.

Eyebrows were raised, but no one said anything.

The Rabbit was the first to break the silence. "I just take my nine tricks," he announced. "Two clubs, two spades and the five hearts."

"And what if the hearts don't break?" asked the Hog.

R.R. looked at him suspiciously. There was a catch somewhere, but he could count up to nine as well as any man, when he took the trouble, and he wasn't going to be talked out of it.

"The hearts? Of course they'll break," he countered defiantly. "I mean, they do usually, don't they?"

"In the event of a very unlucky 5-1 heart split," observed O.O., "there is still the chance of bringing down the king of clubs."

"Alternatively, there may be an endplay," suggested C.C.

"And, anyway," went on the Owl, "you can hardly guard against the remote chance of a 5-1 heart break by going on with the clubs and risking the far more likely 4-2 split. That would kill the contract stone dead."

The Rabbit nodded vigorously. "Quite true, Oscar. Hearts break much better than clubs. I've seen it time and again."

"Papa found the right solution," said the Hog. "When the queen of clubs held, he played a low club away from the ace, retaining control of the suit and giving himself the extra chance of a 3-3 club break in case of bad luck with the hearts. Here's the deal in full.

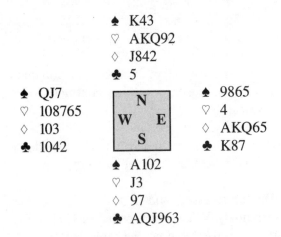

```
              ♠ K43
              ♡ AKQ92
              ◇ J842
              ♣ 5
  ♠ QJ7         N        ♠ 9865
  ♡ 108765   W     E     ♡ 4
  ◇ 103                  ◇ AKQ65
  ♣ 1042        S        ♣ K87
              ♠ A102
              ♡ J3
              ◇ 97
              ♣ AQJ963
```

"And, naturally," said the Corgi, raising a supercilious eyebrow, "you congratulated Papa warmly on an elegant play without which this seemingly foolproof contract can't be made."

A Cumbersome Ace

The Hideous Hog didn't hear him. He was busily writing down another hand. "This time," he informed us, "the spotlight is on Karapet, so I show him as South for the sake of convenience, but it's still the same rubber.

North/South Game. Dealer East.

```
              ♠ Q754
              ♡ QJ1098
              ◇ K10
              ♣ K6

                   N
              W         E
                   S

              ♠ A32
              ♡ A
              ◇ AQ985432
              ♣ 9
```

South	West	North	East
			1♣
2◇	Pass	2♡	Pass
4◇	Pass	5◇	All Pass

"The opening lead was the five of clubs. Karapet played low from dummy and East, winning with the ten, continued with the ace of clubs. How do we bring home the contract?" The Hog turned invitingly to Oscar whose glass of Madeira he raised slowly to his lips.

"If East has the doubleton king of spades ..." mused the Owl.

"Or if either defender has the bare knave of diamonds ..." suggested the Corgi.

H.H. shook his head. "No," he said, "there's nothing quite so convenient, but you can expect to find every card where it should be on the bidding and there's no catch of any kind."

"I lead out all those endless diamonds," said the Rabbit. "Someone's sure to throw the wrong thing sooner or later and be sorry for it afterwards. It's the sort of thing that happens all the time."

"No good," the Hog assured him. "West throws four hearts, then a club, and now East can count every suit, so he knows that he must keep three spades. Karapet, however, made quite certain of the contract."

After a suitable pause, the Hog resumed. "On the ace of clubs, at trick two, he threw the ace of hearts. Now nothing could go wrong for whichever card East played next, declarer would have an extra entry in dummy, allowing him to set up the hearts for two spade discards. In the event, East led a trump, but it made no difference, of course. A club or a spade would have been just as bad, for East was marked with the two missing kings on the bidding.

"These were the four hands."

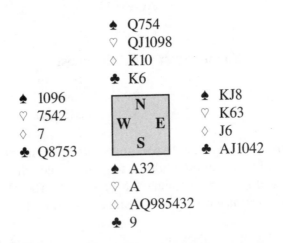

```
                  ♠ Q754
                  ♡ QJ1098
                  ◊ K10
                  ♣ K6
    ♠ 1096        ┌─────────┐      ♠ KJ8
    ♡ 7542        │    N    │      ♡ K63
    ◊ 7           │  W   E  │      ◊ J6
    ♣ Q8753       │    S    │      ♣ AJ1042
                  └─────────┘
                  ♠ A32
                  ♡ A
                  ◊ AQ985432
                  ♣ 9
```

"And it goes without saying," ventured the Corgi, "that you congratulated Karapet on his brilliant dummy play."

Declarer Reversal

"Certainly," replied H.H., "that is, I would have done so, I assure you, but as a matter of fact I, er, retouched the picture a little to bring out my point about overcoming the limitations imposed by nature. It was Karapet, not Papa, who played the first hand and Papa, not Karapet, who was declarer on the last one."

O.O. hooted softly. R.R.'s left ear twitched nervously.

"You see, of course, what this reversal of roles implies," pursued the Hog, satisfied that no one saw anything. "Neither Papa nor Karapet was, in fact, playing above his handicap. Take the Armenian first. We all know that he is the unluckiest player in the Western Hemisphere ..."

"And elsewhere, too, no doubt," broke in the Corgi. "Everyone knows about the evil spell cast by the witch of Ararat in 1462 or thereabouts. Nothing has gone right for the Djoulikyans since."

"Precisely," agreed the Hog. "No finesse ever comes off for Karapet. No suit ever breaks tolerably. So that 5-1 heart split, which anyone else would regard as remote, becomes quite a likely division with Karapet at the wheel. He fully expected it, so we cannot give him the same credit for his far-sighted play as we should give Papa. After all, if you know from experience that it always rains when you go out, it's only natural that even in brilliant sunshine you should take with you an umbrella.

"Now turn to that last hand," continued the Hog. "The discard of the ace of hearts at trick two is a fine, imaginative play – for anyone, that is, except Papa. In the case of our friend Themistocles, nothing comes to him more naturally than throwing aces. Whether it helps or not is a detail. The means justifies the end. Partner gasps. The kibitzers are bewildered and Papa is intoxicated with his own cleverness. And after all," concluded the Hog, "there is no reason to congratulate a man just because he gets intoxicated, is there?"

"What a pity," said the Corgi sadly, "that we must be denied the opportunity to praise your own play, H.H. But since it is always perfect there is nothing you can do to surpass yourself, is there?"

"Here's to humility," said H.H. softly, raising an empty glass.

Chapter Twenty
Facts v. Figures

"When I take a fifty-fifty chance, I expect it to come off eight or nine times out of ten." The Hideous Hog was the speaker. Over dinner at the Griffins he was exposing some of the basic frailties of arithmetic.

"What is a percentage play?" he asked rhetorically.

"It ..." began Oscar the Owl.

"It's nothing of the kind," countered the Hog fiercely. "A percentage play is something that would be fractionally better than something else if other things were equal. But where and when, I ask you," cried H.H., "have other things ever been equal?"

"Just try finding something equal to that Rabbit," he added bitterly. "Then talk to me about percentages."

For nearly thirty seconds there was silence interrupted only by the soft slither of an *œuf Lucullus* down the Hog's capacious gullet. Then, when nothing remained within range, he wrote down this hand on the back of the menu.

Love All. Dealer West.

```
                ♠ K1092
                ♡ 1043
                ◊ KQJ2
                ♣ AK

              ┌─────────┐
              │    N    │
              │  W   E  │
              │    S    │
              └─────────┘

                ♠ A876
                ♡ QJ
                ◊ 10987
                ♣ J32
```

West	North	East	South
1♡	Dble	Pass	1♠
2♡	2♠	Pass	4♠
All Pass			

"Who was declarer?" asked Oscar the Owl.

"And who was West?" enquired Peregrine the Penguin.

"It's quite immaterial," replied H.H. "But if you must know, Papa was West and Colin the Corgi was South. Yes, you can assume a reasonable standard. Colin, of course, is especially good," he added with unaccustomed generosity.

"West," he went on, "led the king of hearts, then the ace, declarer following with the queen and knave. East found the two, but on the second round he showed out, parting with a small diamond. West continued with a third heart to dummy's ten. This East ruffed with the three and South overruffed with the six. Declarer's first concern was with trumps. He led the seven to the king, picking up West's knave on the way, then a low one from dummy. And now," went on the Hog, "we come to the climacteric of the hand. East followed to the second round of trumps with the five. Well, what should declarer do? Should he finesse or go up with his ace, hoping to drop the queen? As you can see, the contract hinges on that."

Peregrine puffed out his chest before speaking. Every day, I thought he looked more and more like a penguin. The black sleeves, the dark orange tie against the broad expanse of a white shirt, all heightened the bird-like effect of his appearance, to which he owed his nickname.

"If it is a percentage play," he began, "a four-one break will materialise twenty-eight times per hundred."

Something which sounded like "nuts" came from H.H. It was hard to say what it was, for his powerful jaws were still locked victoriously in a battle with a portion of salmon, but there was no doubt that he meant to be disparaging. With a little splutter he turned to Oscar.

"Since Papa false-cards continuously," said the Owl, "I am a trifle suspicious of that knave. With queen-knave he would be more likely to throw the queen. On the theory of restricted choice, however ..."

"Quite beside the point," broke in the Hideous Hog. "Papa falsecards as a matter of routine, and can, therefore, afford the occasional true card by way of deception. Anyway, it's irrelevant. As for your 28 per cent," he went on with a contemptuous look at Peregrine, "just consider. West has shown up with seven hearts and we must give him credit for the ace of diamonds to justify his two bids. That's eight cards and we know of three clubs ..."

The Hog paused to see if his words registered. The Penguin and the Owl nodded sagely, a sure sign that they didn't understand.

With a superior snort, the Hog explained: "If West had fewer than three clubs, his partner would have started with six, and if so, he would have surely bid two clubs when North doubled one heart. Now get back to West and add three clubs to the other nine cards he is known to hold, seven hearts, the ace of diamonds and the knave of spades. Only one card is left, so it follows that either the knave of spades or the ace of diamonds must be a singleton."

"In fact," observed Oscar, "that 28 per cent chance is really a fifty-fifty proposition."

"*Ceteris paribus*," added the erudite Penguin.

"*Ceteris* is never *paribus,*" thundered the Hog. "Nothing like it. For one thing, West may have not three clubs but four, in which case his spade must be a singleton and no *ceteris* about it ..."

"Any moment," broke in the Penguin, "you will prove that twenty-eight is more than a hundred."

"And so it is," affirmed H.H., "and you would see it plainly enough if your vision were not obscured by the mirage of percentages. Forget the figures and face the facts. Think of the play. After taking the first two tricks with his top hearts, West led another. Why," cried the Hog, "who but an advanced lunatic would do that, exposing partner to a lethal overruff, if he himself had a singleton knave of trumps? Wouldn't it amount to trump promotion in reverse, an act of sheer sabotage? Only a maniac ..."

"Well, why *did* he lead a third heart?" Interjected Oscar.

"Because he hoped to find partner with the eight of trumps," answered H.H. "It was the only important card he could have and West was quite right to play him for it – but only, of course, if he himself held the queen-knave. With a singleton that shot would make no sense whatever."

"And declarer worked it all out, drew the right inferences and played accordingly?" asked the Penguin suspiciously.

"He did," replied H.H.

"He went up with the king, dropped West's queen and lived happily ever after?" persisted Peregrine.

"On the contrary," retorted the Hideous Hog, "West's knave was a singleton. I went up with the king and ..."

"You did? I thought you said that Colin ..." began Oscar.

"Not wishing to prejudice you, I told a white lie," confessed H.H. "I was declarer."

"But why ..." started the Penguin.

"Why did West play like an advanced lunatic? Because West was that demented Rabbit," replied the Hog.

"I suppose," ventured Oscar the Owl, "that he wanted to kill dummy's ten, not realising that declarer could have nothing to discard."

"Not even that," said H.H. with feeling. "He just miscounted the hearts. Thinking that I had another, it did not dawn on him that his partner would be overruffed." And with a bitter snort he added: "That Rabbit! You know the verger in Somerset Maugham's story, the chap who made a million because he was illiterate? Well, your Rabbit makes thousands of points just because he can't count up to three."

These were the four hands.

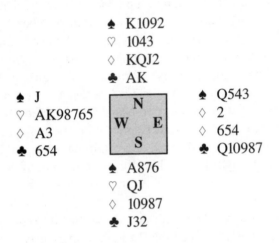

```
              ♠ K1092
              ♡ 1043
              ◇ KQJ2
              ♣ AK
  ♠ J                        ♠ Q543
  ♡ AK98765     N            ♡ 2
  ◇ A3        W   E          ◇ 654
  ♣ 654         S            ♣ Q10987
              ♠ A876
              ♡ QJ
              ◇ 10987
              ♣ J32
```

R.R.'s Percentage Play

A happy twinkle came into the Hog's eye. Evidently, he had thought of some painful episode in the life of one of his many enemies. "I must tell you a hand," he began. Then, noticing our empty plates, he turned to me. "Since I am the only one with a second helping, perhaps you'd better tell them. You see," he added by way of explanation, "I am on a rigorous diet. That is, I am starting tomorrow and it's dangerous to do that sort of thing on an empty stomach.

"You know the hand I mean? That three no-trumps which upset Papa so much last night. Ha! Ha!"

Love All. Dealer East.

♠ AJ10
♡ 985
◊ AKQ
♣ 10875

♠ K42
♡ K76
◊ J42
♣ QJ92

East	South	West	North
Papa	*R.R.*	*S.B.*	*W.W.*
Pass	1NT	Pass	3NT
All Pass			

On the face of it, the Rabbit's opening no-trump may appear to be unusually light, but as he said himself: 'It's just routine. With a balanced thirteen count and no four-card suit, what else can one say?'

Should some purist object to the Rabbit's addition, I should, perhaps, explain that it was his sense of symmetry, rather than his arithmetic, which led him astray. When he first sorted out his hand and began to count his points, the spades were on the left, next to the clubs. To improve the pattern, making the red cards alternate with the black, he transferred the spades to the other side. The count was still in progress as he did it, with the result that the king of spades became worth six points, three when it was on the left with the clubs and three more when it joined the hearts on the right.

The Emeritus Professor of Bio-Sophistry, known to us all as the Secretary Bird, opened the six of clubs, 'looking for his partner's suit', as he put it.

Papa won the trick with the king, followed with the ace and got off play with the three of clubs on which the Secretary Bird threw an inconspicuous diamond.

The Rueful Rabbit pondered, looked at the ceiling for inspiration and sadly shook his head. Then, mumbling something about percentages, he finessed the spade, playing West for the queen. The finesse came off and a few second later the king of hearts gave him his ninth trick, for this was the full deal:

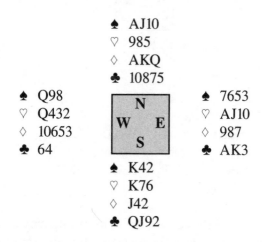

That there should be so much injustice in the world made Papa very angry. "You cannot help your infernal luck," he said to the Rabbit, "but with no indication either way, what made you finesse the spade as you did? Suppose I had the queen? Surely the last thing you wanted was a heart through your king."

"It's a percentage play," explained R.R. "There's a theory that owing to the way the tricks are picked up on one deal, the queen is likely to be under the knave on the next. Or perhaps it's over the knave. I am not sure, but one way is better than the other. So, you see, I gave myself an extra chance and ..."

Seeing the look of disgust on the Greek's face, his voice trailed off. Evidently he had said the wrong thing and that was even worse, of course, than playing the wrong card.

"Can't see what the fuss is about," boomed Walter the Walrus.

"I had fourteen and two tens, so we must have had twenty-seven between us, ample for game."

The Hideous Hog, who was waiting to cut in, laughed uproariously.

"What appeals so much to your fine sense of humour?" asked the Secretary Bird, hissing venomously. "Has anyone slipped and broken a leg?"

"It *is* a percentage play, though none of you can see it. That's what's so funny," answered H.H., chortling. Other people's misfortunes always stimulated him, especially Papa's, and if anything could add to the enjoyment it was the thought that the Secretary Bird was at the receiving end at the same time.

"Can't you see," he went on, "that West was marked with the queen of spades? That's only because you don't realise that the key to the hand was the ace of hearts."

"Hearts had not been touched," protested Papa.

"Of course not," agreed the Hog, "but somebody had the ace, for all that, and that somebody could only be you ..."

"I could ..." hissed the Secretary Bird.

"No, no, of course you couldn't," continued the Hideous Hog, brushing aside the interruption. "Unless Papa had the ace of hearts the contract could not be made at all, and to play a hand on the assumption that it's 100 per cent impossible is the worst percentage play of all. Assume, then, that Papa has the ace of hearts. Now do you see? He has shown up with the ace and king of clubs and that, as Walter will tell you, comes to eleven points. The queen of spades would bring it to thirteen, and how often does Papa pass on that much? Once in fifty deals, perhaps. In other words, at most 2 per cent of the time. So our friend was actually backing a 98 per cent chance. That's what I call a percentage play. No *paribus* about that."

Right Side of an Equation
"But what happens when there are no 98 per cent chances to be had?" objected Peregrine. "Suppose you must choose between two even chances?"

"Then," replied the Hog, "I pick the one that's more even than the other. Let me show you a hand," went on H.H., looking round for a bit of paper.

"Excuse me," he said to the diner at the next table, appropriating his menu, "I recommend the salmon." He then proceeded to write down this hand.

Game All. Dealer West.

♠ K1086
♡ A7
◊ AJ10876
♣ 2

```
      N
   W     E
      S
```

♠ J97
♡ Q106542
◊ Q9
♣ KQ

West	North	East	South
W.W.	*R.R.*	*C.C.*	*H.H.*
3♣	3◊	Pass	3♡
Pass	3♠	Pass	3NT
All Pass			

"For my sins, I cut the Rabbit," said H.H., "but observe that I gave him every chance to raise my hearts by bidding no-trumps. I never play a selfish game, as you know. Naturally, I took his spade bid as an attempt to steer the final contract into my hand. That he actually had a spade suit came as a bit of a surprise, though mind you that's neither here nor there, for unless I was to play the hand I had not enough for game, anyway."

H.H. turned to the play.

"The Walrus opened the six of clubs to Colin's nine and my queen. I led my queen of diamonds and caught Walter's king. That was the second trick. Well, what would you do next? No catches."

The Hog sat back with the air of a conjurer, who had shown that he had nothing up his sleeves.

"We may assume, I think," began the Owl cautiously, "that since our friend the Walrus has shown up with the ace of clubs, by inference, and also with the king of diamonds, he can hardly have any other high cards."

The argument was sound. Walter would be the last man in the club to pre-empt if he had enough for a one bid.

With a graceful snort, H.H. turned to invite Peregrine's opinion.

"I play off the diamonds and watch the discards," answered Peregrine, after giving the matter due consideration. "What happens?"

"Nothing much," answered H.H., "except that defeat is now certain. 100 per cent certain, I should say, so you can call it a percentage play, if you like."

With the air of a schoolmaster, lecturing a class of quarter wits, the Hog proceeded to analyse the hand.

"You can see eight tricks – six diamonds, a club and a heart, but no hope of a ninth without letting in the other side.

"Is the situation, then, desperate? Before saying 'yes', look carefully at the opening lead, the six of clubs. What does that mean? If West's clubs had been headed by the ace-knave-ten, he would have surely led the knave, the top of an interior sequence. Since he didn't, we may assume he was missing one or other of these cards or both.

"Which one?" went on the Hog. "It's not much of a riddle, you know. Had East started with the nine and knave, but no ten, he would have played the knave, not the nine. Therefore, he has the ten. What else? To conform to the rule of eleven he must have one other card better than the six of clubs. Can that card be the eight? Hardly. With the ten-nine-eight he would have played the eight. That leaves two possibilities for East's holding: the knave-ten-nine or the ten-nine-seven. One or the other, and that is your even-money chance. And now, of course, it is all as plain as a pikestaff, isn't it?"

The Hideous Hog raised a bristly eyebrow sarcastically.

"No? You surprise me. Let me put it to you that if East's clubs are ten-seven, there is nothing to be done. The contract cannot be fulfilled. But if East started with the knave-ten-nine, the suit will be blocked, though only if it is played at once. Not otherwise."

During the pause which followed these words, the diner at the next table turned to us to ask, diffidently, if he could have a look at his menu. He wanted to see if *gâteau Savarin* was on that night.

"No," said the Hog sharply. He did not like to be interrupted, and he showed as much. There was really no excuse for bad manners.

Clearing his throat, H.H. recapitulated. "I won the opening lead with my queen of clubs, finessed the diamond, catching Walter's king, and came back to my hand with the nine of diamonds. Now I played the king of clubs, yes, straight into the jaws of West's seven-card suit. You will observe that the defence is now helpless.

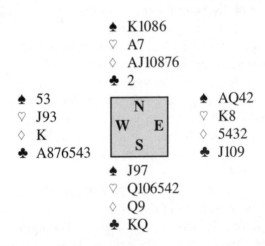

♠ K1086
♡ A7
◇ AJ10876
♣ 2

♠ 53   ♠ AQ42
♡ J93   ♡ K8
◇ K   ◇ 5432
♣ A876543   ♣ J109

♠ J97
♡ Q106542
◇ Q9
♣ KQ

"West can lead a spade through dummy's king or a heart or another club, but I am bound to come to nine tricks and the defence can take no more than four – two clubs and two spades or two clubs, a spade and a heart."

With a courtly bow, H.H. returned the menu to our neighbour, placing it by his coffee cup. Then he resumed: "You can see now why it would have been fatal to play off the diamonds. East would have seized the opportunity to unblock the clubs and my only hope would have disappeared.

"Of course, had East's clubs been the ten-nine-seven, instead of the knave-ten-nine, as they might well have been, my play would have cost 400 instead of 100. As it was, I made a game, worth roughly 600. My even-money chance proved to be two to one in my favour. That is as it should be, for one side of an equation is always a good deal better than the other. The moral of it all is: stick to the facts and let the figures take care of themselves."

Chapter Twenty-One
Nostradamus Speaks

"I'll venture a tenner on the defence," announced R.R.

"I fancy declarer's chances better," said Walter the Walrus, "but a fiver will do me. I don't trust those writer fellows all that much, you know." We were sitting at the bar, poring over a new bridge feature, entitled *Clairvoyant's Corner*, in a glossy magazine.

"It's an original and exciting competition " explained the Rabbit in answer to my enquiry. "You bet with yourself, choosing your own stakes, and if you win, you can pick anything advertised on the page opposite. Every item has been selected from a catalogue of a famous London store. All you have to do is to answer a few simple questions, and what's more, you can double up as you go, hand after hand. There's no limit to what you can win and if you lose, it doesn't really matter, because you are losing to yourself. It's a splendid idea!" This was the first problem:

Love All. Dealer West.

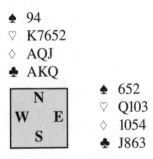

```
            ♠ 94
            ♡ K7652
            ◇ AQJ
            ♣ AKQ
                          ♠ 652
            N             ♡ Q103
        W       E         ◇ 1054
            S             ♣ J863
```

West	North	East	South
Pass	1♡	Pass	1NT
Pass	3NT	Pass	Pass
Pass			

Competitors were given the play to the first two tricks. West opens the queen of spades, declarer wins with the ace and plays the two of diamonds. West follows with the seven and the trick is taken by dummy's knave. At trick three declarer leads dummy's two of hearts. Competitors were invited to answer two questions:

1. Will declarer make his contract?
2. Which tricks will East/West make?

The winners were advised to lose no time in looking up the answers before sending their cheques to Nostradamus, the Competition Editor.

"Why should you think that North/South won't make three no-trumps?" asked the Walrus, turning to the Rabbit. "They must have 25-26 points, maybe more, and every suit is guarded, so what's to stop them?"

"A ruff," jeered the Hideous Hog, who had strolled over in search of a glass.

"The key to the hand," explained R.R. earnestly, "is that the question is pitched in the middle of trick three. East must follow to the two of hearts and of course he plays the queen and ..."

"Why?" broke in W.W. "Everyone knows that second hand should play low. Why should East act unnaturally by going up with the queen?"

"I don't know *why*," replied the Rabbit impatiently, "but what does it matter, so long as it's the right answer. You've just said yourself that it's unnatural and you don't expect to win competitions by being natural, do you? The queen's the last card you'd really play, so it must be the one they want, and if it is, it follows that it must defeat the contract for otherwise it wouldn't be the right card, would it? It's quite simple, you see, and ..."

As R.R. prattled on, he turned over the pages in search of the answer. With a whoop of triumph he read it out: "'Best defence breaks the contract. East plays the queen of hearts.' Didn't I tell you? There's a lot more and a footnote recommending one of several luxury hampers. Better luck next time, Walter, but you can help me choose my hamper. I think I'll have the one with the pintado, in aspic, the *foie gras aux truffes de Périgord*, the peaches in brandy ..."

The Hog, who had been strangely silent for nearly a minute, turned to the Rabbit. "No doubt, R.R.," he said caressingly, "you'll be tempted to double up on the second question."

"N-no," replied the Rabbit. "I think I'll stick to that hamper."

"If you like," coaxed the Hog, "I'll go halves with you and when we win, you can choose the prize, another hamper perhaps. You can take charge of everything. I shan't mind a bit."

"Very well then." The Rabbit knew when he was on to a good thing and he agreed with alacrity. "After all, I suppose, in a sense, I'm playing with their money. Tell me, which tricks will East/West take?"

"The ace and queen of hearts and three spades," said the Hog.

"Why?" asked the Walrus. "Why shouldn't that clever, clever queen of yours fall under declarer's ace? And how do you know what spades West has? You are just guessing, aren't you?"

"On the contrary," replied H.H., "every card is clearly marked. Since West's lead was the queen of spades, declarer must have the king, as well as the ace – a poor false card that ace, but let it pass. What matters is that South can't have another ace, for that would bring his count up to eleven, too much for a response of one no-trump. So, you see, East knows that the queen of hearts will hold and he goes up, not just because it's unnatural, but also because he must clear those spades while partner retains the ace of hearts as an entry. Observe that unless East remembers to forget all about that second-hand-low folklore, the contract is unbeatable.

"As for the length of West's spades, he must have five precisely. We've established that he has the ace of hearts and king of diamonds, since no one else has them, if he also had six spades headed by the queen-knave-ten – oh yes, he must have the ten, for the nine's on view – he would have surely opened the bidding. Alternatively, he would have come in with two spades over one no-trump. One way or another there would have been some squeak from him."

"He could have four spades," insisted the Walrus.

"That would leave South with four spades, too, and with ♠AKxx his response to one heart would have been one spade, not one no-trumps. Show him the full deal, R.R."

These were the four hands:

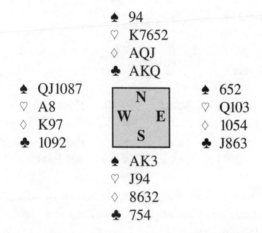

```
                    ♠ 94
                    ♡ K7652
                    ◇ AQJ
                    ♣ AKQ
  ♠ QJ1087                        ♠ 652
  ♡ A8         ┌──────────┐       ♡ Q103
  ◇ K97        │    N     │       ◇ 1054
  ♣ 1092       │  W   E   │       ♣ J863
               │    S     │
               └──────────┘
                    ♠ AK3
                    ♡ J94
                    ◇ 8632
                    ♣ 754
```

"Yes, that's it. Nostradamus had got it right. I agree." The Hog snorted in approval. "You can order another hamper for us, R.R. Try the one with the Yorkshire ham, the lobster flan, the Beluga, the ..."

"We must think of poor Walter," broke in the Rabbit. "Why should he be the only loser? I don't think it's fair."

The Hog nodded sympathetically. "I quite agree. It's all wrong. If you like, Walter," he added, in a burst of generosity, "you can have double or quits with me."

"One doesn't like losing one's money to some mountebank one's never seen ..." began the Walrus doubtfully.

"Losing it to *me*, I mean, er, winning it back from me, would be very different, wouldn't it?" cajoled the Hog. "Looks pretty easy, too, that next problem," he added, covering up the page with his podgy hands to stimulate curiosity. The Walrus yielded reluctantly and we turned to deal number two.

The Rule of One

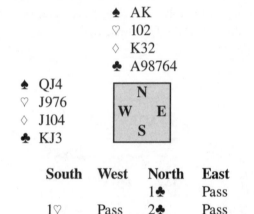

♠ AK
♡ 102
◇ K32
♣ A98764

♠ QJ4
♡ J976
◇ J104
♣ KJ3

South	West	North	East
		1♣	Pass
1♡	Pass	2♣	Pass
2NT	Pass	3NT	All Pass

The Rabbit put away his pen. Having filled in the coupon for the hampers and made out his cheque to Nostradamus, he leant over to read aloud the directions.

"West opens the knave of diamonds on which the two is played from dummy. East's card is the nine and the trick is taken by the queen of diamonds in the closed hand. At trick two the two of clubs is led to West's three, dummy's four and East's ten. East continues with the eight of hearts which declarer wins with the ace. Three tricks have gone and declarer is on play. He leads the five of clubs."

After pausing to digest this information, the Rabbit read on slowly. "If the defenders slip up, declarer makes ten tricks. If declarer slips up, he makes eight tricks.

1. How many tricks will each side win if neither side slips up?
2. How many diamonds has East?"

Sorely perplexed, the Rueful Rabbit came to a halt.

"Crystal clear," declared the Hog, taking over, "and I see that Nostradamus draws the reader's attention to a handsome rose bowl priced at no more than £19.99. So, you see, Walter, if you should double your stake on the first question and invest your winnings on the second, you will not only recover your fiver and acquire the rose bowl, but you will make a small profit into the bargain. Now may I suggest that you step up ..."

"No, no, no," cried the Walrus, trying to keep his voice down to a bellow. "I can't make head or tail of the questions and I am not going to throw good money after bad. How can I tell what slips they won't make when I don't know what they haven't got? And what have East's diamonds to do with it all, anyway?"

With a proud, defiant gesture the Hog put down my glass. "No, Walter," he said softly, "I am not prepared to take your money without giving you a good run for it. Try again. Follow the hand through with me, card by card. By now, of course, you can place every pip. Three tricks have gone and it is West's turn to play to South's five of clubs. Go on from there."

"No doubt," rejoined the Walrus irritably, "West follows suit. The knave of clubs. Your turn."

"Out for a duck," said the Hog sadly, "yet there were only two cards to choose from. I wonder how it is, Walter, that you always manage to pick those odds-on losers."

"Do you mean," asked W.W. incredulously, "that West should play the king of clubs?"

"I knew you'd get there in two," said H.H. "Yes, the Rule of One calls for the king. You can see six clubs in dummy. West had three. Declarer has produced two and East has followed once. That leaves one club out and that club is the queen. Well, who has it? You haven't. Dummy hasn't, and declarer would hardly have played as he did with queen-five-three of clubs. Now you see it all, don't you?"

"Of course," declared R.R. W.W. growled.

"Oh well," sighed the Hog, "in that case I shall have to dot the i's and cross the t's. If West plays the knave, as Walter wants him to do, declarer will duck in dummy and East will win the trick with his lone queen, and whatever he returns declarer will end up with ten tricks – four clubs, two spades, three hearts and one diamond."

"Why *three* hearts?" asked W.W. suspiciously. "Why shouldn't East have the queen or the king, for that matter?"

"Because," replied the Hog – looking out of the corner of a beady eye at the list of prizes – "South is marked with the ace-king-queen of hearts. We've seen East's nine of diamonds at trick one, proclaiming the ace, and we've just established that he has the queen of clubs, too. That accounts for all the missing high cards – except the three top hearts and the queen of diamonds. South needs them all for his two no-trump response. East's lead of the eight of hearts fits in with it, of course – not that we need any confirmation. And now you can see clearly why declarer makes ten tricks if the defence slips."

The Walrus could see clearly that he had somehow lost £10.

The Rule of Two

"And what's declarer's slip?" asked the Rabbit.

"That's the Rule of Two," explained the Hog. "There are two cards declarer cannot see, the king of clubs and queen of clubs. He might go up mistakenly with dummy's ace and play another club, hoping to find East with the king."

"And for all any of you know, he may well have the king," declared the Walrus belligerently.

"True," conceded H.H., "but if it's bare it will drop on the ace and that won't do declarer any good, for on the next round West will come in with the queen and lead a diamond through dummy. And if East's king isn't bare, he must have the queen behind it, so there's nothing to lose by ducking.

"Naturally," went on H.H., "South can't slip unless West slips first. But if both slip, declarer will lose on the deal and end up with no more than eight tricks. And now, of course, the last question answers itself. Money for old rope. If Walter feels like ..."

"No, he certainly doesn't," roared the Walrus, "not another penny."

"Come to think of it," mused the Rueful Rabbit, "how can one tell whether East has five diamonds or four or three, for that matter? No," R.R. added hastily, noting the Hog's ingratiating smile. "I'm not betting any more, not even if you agree to take all my winnings. I wouldn't know what to do with half a third hamper, anyway. It's only that I'd like to know about those diamonds."

"Oh, very well, I'll tell you," said the Hog resignedly. "We're informed that if declarer slips he will make eight tricks. Now if East has five diamonds he will make four of them. The defence must also take two clubs, leaving declarer with seven tricks, not eight. And if East had three diamonds declarer would make nine tricks, even if he slipped, for the suit would be blocked. Having seen East's loud signal with the nine of diamonds at trick one, declarer would play low on the second round and the defence would be confined to four tricks – two clubs, the ten and the king, and two diamonds, the ten and the ace."

We looked up the answers. These were the four hands:

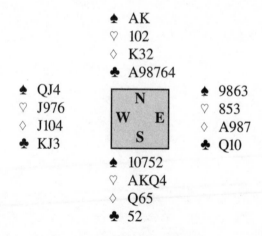

```
                ♠ AK
                ♡ 102
                ◇ K32
                ♣ A98764
♠ QJ4          ┌─────────┐      ♠ 9863
♡ J976         │    N    │      ♡ 853
◇ J104         │ W     E │      ◇ A987
♣ KJ3          │    S    │      ♣ Q10
               └─────────┘
                ♠ 10752
                ♡ AKQ4
                ◇ Q65
                ♣ 52
```

In a smooth purring voice, the Hog addressed the Walrus. "It's a pity, Walter," he said, "that you didn't take advantage of my offer to double up on those last questions. We could have won a bottle of Bollinger. Now you've dropped a tenner with nothing to show for it. Never mind. You can take up for me that special offer of three bottles of old Armagnac and I'll give you one of them. Well call it a consolation prize. Next time, perhaps, you will have more confidence in me."

"I don't like Armagnac," snapped the Walrus. "As for your Nostradamus," he added as he stalked out of the bar in high dudgeon, "I think he's nothing but a twister."

The Rabbit's nose twitched. He looked worried. "It is all above board, isn't it, H.H.?" he asked uneasily. "I mean, I'd like to know what you really think of this Nostradamus. I, er ..."

"*Think* of him!" cried the Hideous Hog. "I don't have to think, I *am* Nostradamus!"